A CLERISY PRESS PRODUCTION

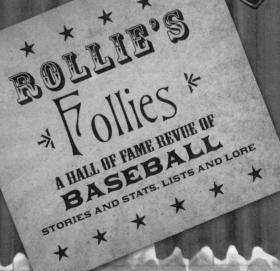

Rollie Fingers
★★★ and *Yellowstone Ritter*

PRESENT

★ ROLLIE'S ★
Follies
⇥ A HALL OF FAME REVUE OF
BASEBALL
STORIES AND STATS, LISTS AND LORE

PUBLISHED BY CLERISY PRESS
1700 MADISON ROAD CINCINNATI, OH 45206
WWW.CLERISYPRESS.COM

ILLUSTRATIONS BY JERRY DOWLING

Interior layout designed by Stephen Sullivan

EDITED BY JACK HEFFRON

LIBRARY OF CONGRESS CATALOGING-IN-PUBLICATION DATA

Fingers, Rollie.
Rollie's follies : a hall of fame revue of baseball lists and lore, stats and stories /
by Rollie Fingers and Yellowstone Ritter.
p. cm.
ISBN-13: 978-1-57860-335-0
ISBN-10: 1-57860-335-8
1. Baseball--United States--Miscellanea. 2. Baseball--United States--History.
3. Baseball--Records--United States. 4. Baseball--United States--Statistics.
5. Baseball players--United States--History. I. Ritter, Yellowstone. II. Title.

GV873.F47 2009
796.3570973--dc22

2008055512

1   2   3   4   5   6   7   8   9   10

Printed in the United States of America
Distributed by Publishers Group West
First edition, first printing

I would like to dedicate this book to all my friends and anyone else who ever put on a pair of spikes. It's amazing that just doing that and walking onto a ball field will bring back memories and take you to a place that you remember from your childhood. You just feel like a youngster again. That's what baseball is all about. I feel that way even today and I'm sixty-two years young. After all, Major League Baseball is nothing more than a kid's game being played by adults.

– Rollie Fingers

CONTENTS

This is a game to be savored, not gulped. There's time to discuss everything between pitches or between innings. – Bill Veeck

Baseball is the only major sport that appears backward in a mirror. – George Carlin

INTRODUCTION

Total strangers ask me questions all the time. It's a big part of my life. After all, I have a waxed moustache and I'm approachable. It's bound to happen.

More often than not, people like to ask me about my playing career. They'll refer to the great times I had with my teammates on the Oakland A's or they will perhaps want to hear one of the more popular anecdotes with which I've been associated. Something tells me I get asked about my infamous World Series strikeout of Johnny Bench more than he does.

Sure, there are questions I get asked over and over for which I have pat answers, but every so often, I'll get asked a question that really intrigues me—to the point that I try and find out the answer for myself.

On any given day, I might hear "Mister Fingers, who is the best current player who has yet to make it into an All-Star Game?

Or I might hear, "Rollie, who is the only Hall of Famer you've faced that you never once managed to get out?"

Let's face it, the answers to these intriguing questions aren't the sort of thing you can look up in your trusty baseball almanac—and that's where this project all started.

I tried to look at baseball information in a new way, through a prism, if you will. I began amassing odd questions, finding out their answers, and then I rounded out the rest of the book with other features that I found to be unusually interesting, weird, or fantastical.

As for the answers to those two trivia questions mentioned above, well, you can find the answers somewhere in the pages ahead.

~ *Rollie Fingers*

THE ROLLIE'S FOLLIES GLOSSARY
By Yellowstone Ritter

Within this here book, you may run into a word from time to time that may seem a bit unusual. Therefore, I've cooked up a glossary. Of course, there may be a word or two on the list below that isn't in existence (before now), but I figure if Billy Shakespeare got to create words out of thin air, then I should be allowed to as well.

centenarian: *an old-timer who has reached the age of one hundred*

combover: *a hairstyle in which hair on one side of a noggin is grown long and then combed over the bald patch*

deliverance: *the act of delivering from restraint, peril, or backwoodsmen*

doh: a cartoonishly exaggerated expression of exasperated regret

dynasty (our definition): *a sports team that has won at least three consecutive championships*

eccentric: *what you would call unusual behavior when it comes from someone who also happens to be a millionaire*

follies: *a series of extraordinary amusements presented with theatrical flair*

football: *a sport in which, oddly enough, the offense is allowed to control the ball*

gargantuanly: *a synonym for ginormously*

gonfalon bubble: *yeah, ummm......, hell, I don't know either!!*

hotbed: *a location conducive to fostering explosive growth*

lathe: *a cutting machine used to shape a piece of wood*

light saver: *a closer who wraps up a game in fewer than 4 outs*

loop-de-loop: *a climbing and diving maneuver by an airborne object*

pawk: *how residents of New England often pronounce the word "park"*

permillage: *like a percentage, only one decimal point more accurate*

phat: *excellent; of excellence*

ratatouille: *a fancy French name for vegetable stew*

Ray: *just like a Devil Ray, only exorcised*

rock maple: *a tough, closed-grain wood sometimes used to make bats*

smelt: *a trout-like cold-water fish that is yummers on the griddle*

spoiler: *someone with no chance of victory who prevents a hopeful from success*

suits: *(my definition) people who make decisions based primarily on money*

tarpaulin: *a normally harmless plastic sheet used to cover and protect things from moisture*

zygotically: *a description for a manner that signifies elements of early development*

Edward Charles Ford

★ ★ ★ No. 19 ★ ★ ★

Whitey Ford

NEW YORK YANKEES — PITCHER

Ht. 5'10"; Wt. 184; Bats Left; Throws Left;
Born Oct. 21, 1928; Home: Lake Success, N. Y.

The 1961 season was Whitey's best with 25
wins and only 4 losses topped off by 2 shutout wins in the World Series. That season
credited him with the Sport Magazine Award
(a Corvette) as MVP in the World Series and
the Cy Young Award as Pitcher of the Year.
He holds the World Series record of most consecutive scoreless innings (33⅔), and most
games won (10) plus many other records. He
pitched in 6 All-Star Games.

EAGUE PITCHING RECORD ★ ★ ★							
Lost	Pcts.	Hits	Runs	ER	SO	Walks	ERA
8	.680	243	90	83	160	69	2.90
71	.711	1954	805	711	1369	890	2.83

DODGERS

SANDY KOUFAX   pitcher

Sanford Braun

angels
30

NOLAN RYAN

CALIFORNIA ANGELS   PITCHER

Lynn Ryan, Jr.

1

ORIGINAL BIRTH NAMES

◇◇

**CHANCES ARE THAT YOUR FAVORITE TEAM USED TO BE CALLED
SOMETHING ELSE. MANY FAMOUS PLAYERS ALSO HAD
A SIGNIFICANTLY DIFFERENT NAME ON THEIR BIRTH
CERTIFICATES. HERE'S A COMBINED LIST THAT TAKES YOU
BACK TO THE ROOTS OF BALL CLUBS AND PLAYERS ALIKE.**

Atlanta Braves...Boston Red Stockings

Baltimore Orioles...Milwaukee Brewers

Yogi Berra..Lawrence Peter Berra

Bert Blyleven..Rik Aalbert Blyleven

Boston Red Sox...Boston Americans

Kevin Brown..James Brown

Roger Clemens..William Clemens

Chicago Cubs...Chicago White Stockings

Cincinnati Reds.....................................Cincinnati Red Stockings

Cleveland Indians...Cleveland Blues

Joe DiMaggio..Giuseppe DiMaggio

J.D. Drew..........................D.J. Drew (David Jonathan Drew)

Whitey Ford...Edward Charles Ford

Nomar Garciaparra...Anthony Garciaparra

Lou Gehrig...Henry Gehrig

Lefty Grove..Robert Moses Grove

Roy Halladay...Harry Leroy Halladay

J.J. Hardy..James Jerry Hardy

Mike Hargrove.....................................Dudley Michael Hargrove

Whitey Herzog.......................Dorrel Norman Elvert Herzog

Houston Astros...Houston Colt .45's

Chipper Jones..Larry Jones

Sandy Koufax...Sanford Braun

Los Angeles Angels of Anaheim.........................Los Angeles Angels

Los Angeles Dodgers......................................Brooklyn Atlantics

Billy Martin..Alfred Manual Martin

Russell Martin.....................................Russell Nathan Coltrane

Milwaukee Brewers...Seattle Pilots

Minnesota Twins..Washington Senators

New York Yankees...Baltimore Orioles

Oakland A's...Philadelphia Athletics

Philadelphia Phillies......................................Philadelphia Quakers

Pittsburgh Pirates..Pittsburgh Alleghenys

J.J. Putz..Joseph Jason Putz

Babe Ruth...George Herman Ruth

Nolan Ryan...Lynn Ryan Jr.

C.C. Sabathia.....................................Carsten Charles Sabathia

San Francisco Giants......................................New York Gothams

St. Louis Cardinals..St. Louis Browns

Casey Stengel..Charles Dillon Stengel

Tampa Bay Rays.......................................Tampa Bay Devil Rays

Texas Rangers..Washington Senators

B.J. Upton...Melvin Emanuel Upton

Arky Vaughan...Joseph Floyd Vaughan

Honus Wagner..John Peter Wagner

Washington Nationals.......................................Montreal Expos

Hoyt Wilhelm..James Hoyt Wilhelm

Follies Factoids

The Baltimore Orioles, Milwaukee Brewers, and the Washington Nationals are all third incarnations.

The first Baltimore Orioles major league ball club played from 1882–1899 whereas the second version cropped up for a single season in 1901.

The initial Milwaukee Brewers major league club played a single year in 1884, whereas the second version played solely in 1891.

The Washington Nationals premiered as a major league club in 1884 and played only one season while the second version of the Nats played from 1886–1889.

Third time's the charm.

2

THE FALLEN SMELT

✕✕

THE FOLLOWING POEM IS BASED ON THE ABSOLUTELY TRUE STORY OF HOW A BASEBALL GAME WAS ONCE INTERRUPTED BY A FISH THAT FELL FROM THE SKY—SMACK DOWN ONTO ST. LOUIS BROWNS HURLER ELLIS KINDER.

May 17, 1947
'Twas a beautiful day at Fenway.
Baseball was well underway.
Boston fans, they were burping.
Local birds? They were chirping.
Well, some of them were anyway.

The Browns were in town for baseball
amidst that gargantuanly massive green wall.
Kinder took to the mound
to hurl that spherical round,
quite unaware that his sky would soon fall.

Nearby in the calm Charles River
Mother Nature—she sure did deliver
a seagull, with a swoop
and a precision loop-de-loop
did pluck from the drink its fish dinner.

4

In its beak held a huge three-pound smelt,
wriggling mad at the hand it'd been dealt.
The gull flew from the dock
then soared o'er Fenway Pawk,
But began wishing his fish to be svelte.

Kinder continued to pitch for St. Louie
unaware of this struggle most screwy.
The gull's jaws did unclick
The smelt dropped like a brick,
smashing onto him like cold ratatouille.

The Splinter's eyesight? Most splendid.
But his faith in them—suspended!!
The day was awry,
a fish had dropped from the sky
—only to crash onto Kinder distended.

The pitcher was quite dumbfounded
at the sight of this smelt freshly grounded.
But he dug in his spikes
and kept throwing those strikes.
In the end, his Browns had rebounded.

But let Kinder's tough lesson be felt,
even if you're a gritty black belt.
There's just always a threat!
You can't guess when YOU'LL get
a welt from being pelted by smelt.

3

JOSE REYES ON THE BASE PATHS

IN 2006, UPON HITTING AN INSIDE-THE-PARK HOME RUN, JOSE REYES OF THE NEW YORK METS WAS CLOCKED RUNNING THIS 120-YARD TREK IN A MERE 14.7 SECONDS.

At this equivalent pace,

~ he would run the length of a football field in 12.25 seconds ~
~ he would run a lap in 53.9 seconds ~
~ he would run a mile in 3 minutes and 35.6 seconds ~
~ he would run 21.55 miles in 60 minutes ~
~ he would run a marathon in 94 minutes and 12.8 seconds ~

AND

~ he would run from CitiField to Citizen's Bank Park
in 6 hours, 38 minutes, and 33 seconds ~

*Imagine how much faster Jose Reyes could sprint if
he didn't have to corner bases.*

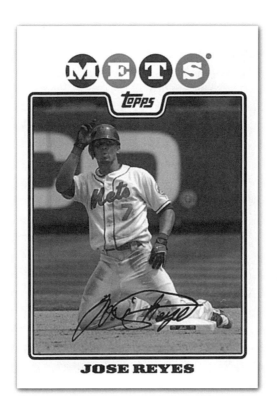

JOSE REYES

Follies Factoid

A trip around the basepaths is 120 yards —the equivalent distance from goalpost to goalpost on a football field.

4

CY AND TY

◇◇

CY YOUNG AND TY COBB ARE TWO OF THE
ELITE LEGENDS OF THE GAME.

EVEN THOUGH HE RETIRED IN 1911, FIREBALLER CY YOUNG
STILL HOLDS THE MAJOR LEAGUE RECORDS FOR VICTORIES,
COMPLETE GAMES, AND INNINGS PITCHED.

EVEN THOUGH TY COBB LAST SHARPENED HIS SPIKES IN 1928,
HE STILL HOLDS THE MAJOR LEAGUE RECORDS FOR MOST
BATTING TITLES (TWELVE) AND FOR HAVING POSTED THE HIGHEST
CAREER BATTING AVERAGE (.367).

HERE IS AN INTERTWINING TIMELINE THAT HIGHLIGHTS THE
MANY MILESTONES OF CY AND TY.

1867	*Denton True Young* is born in rural Ohio.
c. 1879	After completing the sixth grade, *"Dent"* leaves school to work full-time on his family's fifty-four-acre farm.
1886	*Tyrus Raymond Cobb* is born in a cabin in Georgia. His strict father names him after the Phoenician city of Tyre (famous for having so valiantly battled Alexander the Great's mighty army).

1888	*"Farmboy" Young* plays for a local semi-pro team both as a pitcher and infielder.
c. 1893	*Ty Cobb* becomes fascinated with baseball to the point that he takes his homemade bat to bed with him every night.
1898	*Dent Young* tries out for the minor league team in Canton. The catcher who warms up Dent is wildly impressed by his fastball and nicknames him Cyclone, a name that is later shortened to Cy.
1890	At the age of twenty-three, *Cy Young* becomes a major league baseball player (for the now-defunct Cleveland Spiders). His catcher takes to lining the inside of his mitt with steak to help protect himself from Cy's fastball.
1891	*Cy* begins a four-year stretch in which he will pitch in excess of four hundred innings each and every year.
1892	*Cy* hurls 453 innings and racks up 36 wins, both career bests. Over the second half of this season, the Spiders finish in first place, which earns them an automatic berth in the championship series. There, they fail to win a single game against the Boston Beaneaters—a direct ancestor of today's Atlanta Braves.
1893	In large part because of *Cy Young*'s legendary fastball, the pitching distance is moved back to where it currently stands at sixty feet and six inches. With this adjustment, the modern era of baseball is born. Cy continues to excel all the same.
1895	*Cy* begins using a fielding glove. Though the Cleveland Spiders finish in second place, they end up toppling the first-place Baltimore Orioles in the "World's Championship Series." Cy contributes three victories to this victorious Cleveland effort.
1896	*Cy* leads the league in both strikeouts (140) and saves (3). As for *Ty Cobb*, he turns ten years old.
1897	*Cy* pitches his first no-hitter, although he feels it is underserved due to a generous official scorer.

1898	*Cy* plays his ninth and final season for the Cleveland Spiders. Overall, he posted a 241–135 record for them and completed 93.7% of the games that he started.
1899	The owner of the Cleveland Spiders buys a second major league team, the St. Louis Perfectos. He assigns *Cy* and his other stars to play for them instead.
1900	At thirty-three, *Cy* plays his second and final season for the Perfectos. Overall, he posted a 45–35 record for this early incarnation of the St. Louis Cardinals.
1901	*Cy* becomes an original member of the new American League's club in Boston. He wins the triple crown by leading this junior league in victories (33), ERA (1.62), and strikeouts (158).
1902	During the offseason, *Cy Young* puts in time as the pitching coach for the Harvard University baseball team. The public delights in the idea of a hayseed with a sixth-grade education being placed in charge of Ivy League students.
1903	*Cy Young*'s Boston team finishes in first place and goes on to play in the original World Series. There, they beat the great Honus Wagner and the rest of the Pittsburgh Pirates by a tally of five games to three. In this initial Fall Classic, Cy goes 2–1 with a 1.85 ERA and smacks a triple for good measure. Though only seventeen, *Ty Cobb* gains valuable experience in semi-pro ball. He also further develops his side talents for money management and self-promotion.
1904	*Cy Young* pitches the first perfect game of the modern era—and does so at the expense of a taunting rival (Rube Waddell). His Boston team finishes in first place again, but the prospective World Series with John McGraw's New York Giants is cancelled when McGraw refuses to play. McGraw alleges that Boston hails from a vastly inferior league, despite the fact that they defeated the NL champions the previous year.
1904	*Ty Cobb* successfully tries out for the minor league Augusta Tourists. They eventually cut him, but he perseveres and instead catches on with a team in Anniston, Alabama.

1905   A vastly improved *Ty* returns to the Augusta Tourists,
        and in August they sell him to the Detroit Tigers. Later
        that same month, Ty's mother apparently mistakes his
        father for a burglar and kills him. Despite this tragedy,
        Ty debuts for Detroit shortly thereafter. Almost immedi-
        ately, he is a victim of hazing at the hands of the veteran
        players. He cites these "old-timers" for forming him into
        a "snarling wildcat." The Tigers finish in third place, one
        half game in front of *Cy Young*'s Boston Americans.

1906   Demonstrating remarkable control, *Cy Young* only sur-
        renders walks at the rate of 1 per every 11.5 innings.
        Ty Cobb suffers a nervous breakdown and enters a
        sanitarium. Once back on the field, he blossoms into a
        truly superb player. Soon, he is known throughout the
        entire country by the nickname of the "Georgia Peach."

1907   *Cy Young* starts the season as Boston's player-manager.
        However, after six games, he relinquishes the reigns.
        Three others would also manage the underachieving
        ball club that season. During spring training, *Ty* fights
        a groundskeeper and ends up choking the man's wife
        when she tries to intervene. During the regular season,
        Ty steals second base, third base, and home plate on
        successive attempts for the first of many times. Ty
        becomes a pitchman for Coca-Cola (they share the same
        home state of Georgia) and in advertisements, credits the
        soft drink with helping him get through double-headers.
        Ty wins his first batting title. His Tigers finish in first
        place 32.5 games ahead of Boston, but are unable to win
        a single game in the World Series against Three Finger
        Brown and the slick-fielding Chicago Cubs.

1908   Boston changes their team name from the Americans to
        the name we are now more familiar with. *Cy Young* is
        there to wear one of those initial Red Sox uniforms. At the
        age of forty-one, Cy racks up a 21–11 record to go along
        with a 1.26 ERA. In addition, he hurls his third and final
        no-hitter. *Ty* marries the daughter of a very wealthy man.

Yet again, his Detroit Tigers finish in first place (this time 15.5 games ahead of Boston) but for the second year in a row, the Chicago Cubs vanquish them in the World Series.

1909   *Cy Young* is traded from the Red Sox to the Cleveland Naps, a precursor of today's Cleveland Indians. Summarily, Cy wins nineteen games for them. Ty Cobb's Detroit Tigers win their third straight pennant. Ty wins the Triple Crown by leading the league in hitting (.377), home runs (9), and RBIs (107). However, the Tigers go on to lose their third straight World Series, this time to the Pittsburgh Pirates. It would prove to be Ty's final postseason appearance.

1910   *Ty* controversially sits out the last games of the regular season in order to protect his claim to the batting title.

1911   *Cy Young* is now the oldest player in baseball by nearly three years. In midseason, with his abilities winding down, he is released by Cleveland. However, the Boston Rustlers, yet another early version of today's Atlanta Braves, give him a last hurrah. At season's end, he completes his twenty-second year in baseball and retires at the age of forty-four. *Ty Cobb*, at the age of twenty-four, has his best season ever. He hits .420, has 367 total bases, steals 83 more, draws 44 walks, scores 147 runs, and drives in an additional 127. He also enjoys a forty-game hitting streak. He unanimously wins the league MVP award.

1912   While playing New York, *Ty Cobb* goes into the stands to assault a heckler. Cobb is suspended, in part, because the loudmouth was a severely handicapped amputee.

1915   *Ty* is plunked by opposing pitchers on ten different occasions. He steals 96 bases and draws 118 walks. All three of these totals would prove to be career highs for him.

1917   *Ty* is paid $25,000 to star in a Hollywood picture as a bank clerk from Georgia who becomes a great baseball player. The film is roundly panned and one critic calls it pure hokum. On the field, Ty racks up an impressive 24 triples.

1918   During the offseason, *Ty* enlists in the Army. He serves sixty-seven days in France with the Chemical Corps as a captain, teaching enlisted men how to deal with chemical attacks. George Sisler and Christy Mathewson also serve in this "Gas and Flame Division" underneath their major, Branch Rickey.

1919   *Ty* wins his twelfth and final batting title.

1921   At the age of thirty-four, *Ty* becomes the player-manager for the Tigers.

1925   To prove a point at the expense of Babe Ruth, *Ty* announces that he will temporarily swing for the fences. He ends up blasting five home runs in two days. Babe Ruth counters that if he chose to hit for average instead of for power, that he would have hit .600 during the course of his career.

1926   Manager *Ty Cobb* plays his final season in Detroit. In his six seasons as skipper, he ends up thirty-five games above .500, but never guides his team to first place. As a player, even though he only plays in seventy-nine games, he strikes out only twice.

1927   *Ty Cobb* plays for Connie Mack's Philadelphia Athletics. This becomes the team that finishes in second place behind the historic "Murderer's Row" version of the New York Yankees.

1928   At the age of forty-one, *Ty Cobb* plays his twenty-fourth and final season. He earns $85,000, a payday that is dwarfed by the amount of money he is taking in from his various investments.

1933   *Cy* becomes a widower. His remaining years are spent working odd jobs and appearing at baseball functions, particularly in Cleveland.

1936   *Ty Cobb* is voted into the Hall of Fame as part of its initial class. He receives more votes (222) than any of his fellow inductees (Babe Ruth, Honus Wagner, Christy Mathewson, and Walter Johnson). As for Cy Young, he receives only 111 votes in this election and misses the cut.

1937   *Cy Young*, Nap Lajoie, and Tris Speaker are all elected into the Hall of Fame on their second try.

1941   *Ty Cobb* faces off against Babe Ruth in a series of golf tournaments. Ty wins them all.

1955   Back on his Ohio farm, *Cy* dies at the ripe old age of eighty-eight.

1956   The first "Cy Young Award" is given out to honor excellence in pitching. Don Newcombe of the Brooklyn Dodgers becomes the first recipient.

1961   *Ty Cobb* passes away in Atlanta at the age of seventy-four.

1999   *Cy* and *Ty* are both named to the Major League Baseball All-Century Team.

Follies Factoids

Cy Young threw the first pitch in World Series history.

Over the course of Cy's career, 32% of the runs given up by him were unearned.

Cy Young once held seventy-three consecutive batters hitless.

Cy spent 53% of his career playing for the two Cleveland teams and 37% playing for the two Boston clubs.

Cy Young and Roger Clemens both racked up exactly 192 victories for the American/Red Sox franchise.

In 1901, Boston raided Cy Young away from the NL for $3,500. In 2009 dollars, that works out to an annual salary of about $86,500.

In 1908, after a bitter holdout, Ty Cobb signed for $5,000. In 2009 dollars, that works out to an annual salary of about $114,500.

Ty stole home 54 times.

Ty Cobb was credited with helping Joe DiMaggio negotiate his rookie contract with the New York Yankees. Both men were known for being especially prudent with money.

Ty was once kept from choking an umpire after they agreed to a post-game brawl underneath the grandstand.

Ty Cobb at one point owned three Coca-Cola bottling plants.

At the time of his death, Cobb had a net worth of $11.78 million. In 2009 dollars, that works out to a fortune of about $81 million.

5

THE
PHAT ALBERT DOSSIER:
HIS FIRST EIGHT YEARS
(2001-2008)

PUJOLS, Albert

DOSSIER - 5

EARLY CHILDHOOD: Dominican Republic

HIGH SCHOOL YEARS:
Dominican Republic/New York City/Missouri

COLLEGE: Batted .461 at a junior college in the
Kansas City area

SCOUTED: A scout with the Tampa Bay Devil Rays
brought Albert to their attention, but the club
chose not to sign him. The scout quit in protest.

DRAFTED: Was the 402nd pick in the 1999 June draft

PROS DRAFTED AHEAD OF HIM INCLUDED:
Josh Hamilton, Josh Beckett, Barry Zito, Ben
Sheets, Brian Roberts, Carl Crawford, John Lackey,
Justin Morneau, Hank Blalock, J.J. Putz

INDEPENDENT LEAGUE: In lieu of accepting the
Cardinals' bonus offer of $10,000, Albert instead
played in the Jayhawk League until the offer was
increased to $70,000.

MINOR LEAGUE GAMES: 133

PUJOLS, Albert

MOST FREQUENT MINOR LEAGUE HOME:
Peoria, IL

MINOR LEAGUE ACCOMPLISHMENTS: In his only season in the minors, he started out in Class A ball and ended the season in AAA

MLB DEBUT YEAR: 2001

AGE AT DEBUT: 21

ROOKIE YEAR ACCOMPLISHMENTS:
- NL Rookie of the Year
- Silver Slugger
- Finished fourth in NL MVP voting

EARLIEST TEAMMATES INCLUDED: Mark McGwire, Placido Polanco, Bobby Bonilla, Rick Ankiel, Matt Morris, J.D. Drew, Mike Timlin

PRIMARY MANAGER: Tony La Russa

TOTAL MANAGERS PLAYED FOR: 1

TOTAL SEASONS IN THE MAJOR LEAGUES THUS FAR: 8

PUJOLS, Albert

NUMBER OF LOSING SEASONS: 1

STATS DURING HIS FIRST EIGHT YEARS:
.334 BA/319 HR/977 RBI

REGULAR SEASON WINNING PERCENTAGE IN GAMES IN
WHICH PUJOLS PARTICIPATED: 56%

MAJOR LEAGUE AFFILIATIONS:
St. Louis Cardinals (100%)

POSITIONS PLAYED DURING HIS GAMES (rounded):

1B -- 71%	DH -- 1%
LF -- 22%	2B -- 1 game
3B -- 8%	SS -- 1 game
RF -- 3%	

INJURY AND/OR REST RATE: 4%

BEST SEASON:
(2003) .359 BA/43 HR/124 RBI

MOST FREQUENT OPPONENT: Houston Astros

HOME AWAY FROM HOME:
Comerica Park in Detroit (.630 BA/2 HR/5 RBI)

PUJOLS, Albert

MOST FREQUENT FOES:
Roy Oswalt: 76 plate appearances (.314 BA/4 HR/9 RBI)
Ben Sheets: 74 plate appearances (.371/4 HR/11 RBI)
Carlos Zambrano: 62 plate appearances (.259/5 HR/10 RBI)

THE PITCHER HE HOMERED MOST OFTEN AGAINST:
Wade Miller (6)

THE PITCHER HE OWNED:
Chris Capuano
.556 (15 for 27) with 3 HRs, 10 RBIs, 5 walks, and 3
strikeouts.

THE PITCHER WHO OWNED HIM:
No one really meets the criteria although Albert initially went 0 for 10 against reliever Ryan Madson

THE PITCHER HE STRUCK OUT MOST OFTEN AGAINST:
Ben Sheets (14)

BATTING CHAMPIONSHIPS: 1

LEAGUE MVP AWARDS: 2

GOLD GLOVES: 1

FIELDING PERMILLAGE: .991

PUJOLS, Albert

ALL-STAR TEAMS: 7

ALL-STAR STATS:
14 AT-BATS: .429/BA/0 HR/3 RBI

PLAYOFF RECORD:
5 postseasons: 53 games
189 AT-BATS
.323 BA/13 HR/35 RBI
2 pennants 1 world championship

MOST FREQUENT TEAMMATES:
Jim Edmonds: 7 seasons
Jason Isringhausen: 7 seasons

CLOSEST STATISTICAL TWIN: Joe DiMaggio

HALL OF FAME CALIBRE RATING: 137%

6

THE ALL-TIME LEFTY TEAM

<><><><><><><><><><><><><><><><><><><><><><><><><><><><><><><><><><><><>

A TWENTY-FIVE-MAN DREAM ROSTER COMPRISED OF MANY OF THE GAME'S GREATEST LEFT-HANDERS.

MANAGER: Casey Stengel

COACHES: Charley Grimm, Whitey Herzog, Tommy Lasorda, and Chuck Tanner

PITCHING STAFF (Career statistics for many of the game's premiere southpaws, along with the primary ball club they pitched for)

STARTERS AND LONG RELIEVERS

	Won–Loss	ERA	Strikeouts
Steve Carlton (*Phillies*)	329–244	3.22	4,136
Whitey Ford (*Yankees*)	236–106	2.75	1,956
Lefty Grove (*Athletics*)	300–141	3.06	2,266
Randy Johnson (*Mariners*)	295–160	3.26	4,789
Sandy Koufax (*Dodgers*)	165–87	2.76	2,396
Eddie Plank (*Athletics*)	326–194	2.35	2,246
Babe Ruth (*Red Sox*)	94–46	2.28	488
Warren Spahn (*Braves*)	363–245	3.09	2,583
Rube Waddel (*Athletics*)	193–143	2.16	2,316

MIDDLE RELIEVER

	Won–Loss	ERA	Strikeouts
Jesse Orosco (*Mets*)	87–80	3.16	1,179

CLOSERS

	Won–Loss	ERA	Strikeouts	Saves
John Franco (*Mets*)	90–87	2.89	975	424
Billy Wagner (*Astros*)	39–37	2.40	1,066	385

POSITION PLAYERS

Position		AVG	HR	RBI	SB
C	Yogi Berra (*Yankees*)	.285	358	1,430	
1B	Lou Gehrig (*Yankees*)	.340	493	1,995	
2B	Charley Gehringer (*Tigers*)	.320	184	1,427	181
SS	Arky Vaughan (*Pirates*)	.318	96	926	118
3B	George Brett (*Royals*)	.305	317	1,595	201
LF	Barry Bonds (*Giants*)	.298	762	1,996	514
CF	Ty Cobb (*Tigers*)	.366	117	1,937	892
RF	Stan Musial (*Cardinals*)	.331	475	1,951	123
DH	Babe Ruth (*Yankees*)	.342	714	2.217	123

RESERVES

Position		AVG	HR	RBI	SB
C	Bill Dickey (*Yankees*)	.313	202	1,209	
2B	Pete Rose (*Reds*)	.306	119	936	131
SS	Ozzie Smith (*Cardinals*)	.264	5	528	422
CF	Mickey Mantle (*Yankees*)	.281	296	727	102
DH	Ted Williams (*Red Sox*)	.344	521	1,839	102

Barry Bonds, Lou Gehrig, Stan Musial, and Babe Ruth also hold the distinction of having *thrown* left-handed.

Mickey Mantle, Pete Rose, and Ozzie Smith were all switch hitters, but only their left-handed career totals are featured here.

EVEN MORE GREAT SOUTHPAWS
AND LEFTY HITTERS

Who among the following would YOU have included
on the all-lefty team?

Richie Ashburn, Earl Averill, Frank Baker, Dave Bancroft,
Jake Beckley, Carlos Beltran, Wade Boggs, Jim Bottomley,
Dan Brouthers, Jesse Burkett, Max Carey, Rod Carew, Fred Clarke,
Mickey Cochrane, Eddie Collins, Earle Combs, Roger Connor,
Sam Crawford, George Davis, Larry Doby, Johnny Evers, Elmer
Flick, Nellie Fox, Frankie Frisch, Tom Glavine, Lefty Gomez, Goose
Goslin, Ken Griffey Jr., Tony Gwynn, Billy Hamilton, Cole Hamels,
Todd Helton, Harry Hooper, Carl Hubbell, Reggie Jackson, Tommy
John, Chipper Jones, Jim Kaat, Scott Kazmir, Willie Keeler, Chuck
Klein, Mickey Lolich, Sparky Lyle, Heinie Manush, Rube Marquard,
Eddie Mathews, Hideki Matsui, Joe Mauer, Willie McCovey,
Johnny Mize, Joe Morgan, Eddie Murray, Hal Newhouser,
David Ortiz, Mel Ott, Herb Pennock, Jorge Posada, Jose Reyes,
Sam Rice, Eppa Rixey, Ed Roush, C.C. Sabathia, Johan Santana,
Red Schoendienst, Joe Sewell, George Sisler, Enos Slaughter,
Tris Speaker, Duke Snider, Mike Stanton, Willie Stargell, Ichiro
Suzuki, Bill Terry, Sam Thompson, Chase Utley, Lloyd Waner, Paul
Waner, John Ward, Zach Wheat, Carl Yastrzemski, and Ross Youngs

GREAT LEFTY
STAN
"THE MAN"
MUSIAL

Follies Factoids

Stan Musial retired with 3,630 career hits. Oddly, he managed to hit 1,815 at home with the other 1,815 hit on the road.

Pete Rose was an extraordinarily versatile baseball guy. Besides managing 786 games (nearly the equivalent of five full seasons), he spent four seasons as a second baseman, four more as a left fielder, an additional four as a right fielder, yet another four as a third baseman, and ended his playing career by playing eight seasons at first base.

Barry Bonds, baseball's all-time home run king, has tallied more runs in his career than he has RBIs (2,227 to 1,996).

In his twenty-two seasons of playing major league baseball, Barry Bonds has played against every single team save for one— the Cleveland Indians.

7

VINCE COLEMAN
AND THE CARNIVOROUS TARP

◇◇◇

The baseball field is an extremely dangerous place. With no warning, baseballs and splintered bats have flown through the air at dangerously high velocities—even when Roger Clemens wasn't on the mound facing Mike Piazza.

Rare is the pitcher who doesn't fear the comebacker. Even more rare is the hitter who hasn't formed an emotional attachment to his batting helmet.

But numerous other objects can conspire to make the baseball diamond a minefield of horrors. Sharp metal spikes, loose rocks, hidden puddles, discarded catcher's masks, unyielding outfield walls, concrete dugout steps, divots in the grass, and bone-crunching player collisions have all conspired to put the toughest of players on the disabled list.

But only once in history, I repeat *only once*, has a player been done in by tarp.

The year was 1985. The place was St. Louis. At the close of the regular season, Whitey Herzog's Cardinals had literally run their way into a playoff spot. His track team of speedsters tallied up 101 victories and one of the most potent reasons for this success was a young outfielder by the name of Vince Coleman.

On October 13, the Cards were about to host the Los Angeles

Dodgers in Game Four of the NL Championship Series. However, the big game was momentarily postponed due to some precipitation. Now, it was nothing to build an ark over, but nonetheless, the switch had been thrown to roll the mechanical tarpaulin onto the field.

Not wanting to break his routine, Coleman went out onto the tarp and began his normal stretching exercises. He had already swiped an incredible 111 bases that year—and you just have to know that Vince had designs on padding the total.

Eventually, the rain subsided to a light drizzle so the grounds crew made the call to mechanically roll up the tarp. The switch was thrown.

Where was Vince Coleman at the time? He was still on the surface of the tarp. Could Vince be seen by the crew? Nope, the large cylinder was blocking him from view.

He continued stretching out his million-dollar wheels, blithely unaware that he was about to be stretched in an entirely different way. All too quickly, Vince felt a twinge of pain and wheeled around to see that the ever-coiling tarp was on his left knee like a pit bull gnawing on a porterhouse.

The shocked player screamed for help but the mechanism continued up his leg before the crew could cut power. At that point, the crew sprinted out and gently wrested him free from the man-eating cylinder.

Unfortunately, Coleman had suffered a bone chip in his knee. He also endured some severe bruising to his leg and had to be stretchered off the field. Sadly, Vince's season had come to a premature end.

However, St. Louis managed to win the pennant against the Dodgers all the same, even though "Vincent Van Go" had gone and left.

What ended up happening in the 1985 Fall Classic?

Truth be told, there was a happy ending because thousands of Missourians celebrated a World Series Championship. It can even be speculated that these proud fans wouldn't have had cause to celebrate had it not been for Vince's freak injury.

Why is that?

It's because the 1985 World Champions ended up being the cross-state Kansas City Royals—who defeated the somewhat depleted Cardinal team by a margin of four games to three.

As for Vince Coleman, he fully recovered and over the next twelve seasons, he managed to pad his stolen base totals by another 654. But best of all, he never again managed to get eaten by tarp.

Follies Factoids

The St. Louis Cardinals have lost eight World Series, as have their legendary rivals, the Chicago Cubs. The Giants and Dodgers, also legendary rivals, have both lost twelve World Series.

In the 1980s, speed ruled. Not a single player during the decade managed to hit as many as 50 home runs in a season.

THE REDEMPTION SERIES

The 2008 World Series was notable for the fact that it matched up the active franchise with the worst overall winning permillage (Tampa Bay—.417) against the ball club with the most losses in history (Philadelphia Phillies—10,098). But in the end, only the Phillies fully redeemed themselves.

Of the thirteen areas of the United States that had franchises in all four major sports in 2008, Philadelphia had gone the longest without a sports championship of any kind—having last gotten a parade in 1983 thanks to the 76ers.

A TEAM EFFORT: HEROES FROM THE 2008 SERIES
Cole Hamels, the Series MVP, pitched thirteen innings, won a game, and notched 8 strikeouts.

Right fielder **Jayson Werth** knocked out 8 hits and drew 4 walks over the course of the five-game series.

Slugger **Ryan Howard** had 3 homers, drew 3 walks, and drove in 6 of the Phillies' 24 runs.

Starter **Joe Blanton** not only hurled a quality start
but also knocked a homer.

Second baseman **Chase Utley** fielded errorlessly,
drew 5 walks, and smashed 2 home runs.

Relievers **Chad Durbin, Scott Eyre, Brad Lidge,**
and **J.C. Romero** combined for eight scoreless innings,
scattering only 4 hits and 1 walk along the way.

CONSOLATION

The Tampa Bay Rays won the American League pennant
despite having the lowest payroll in the entire league.
Comparatively, the Rays worked with what
amounted to 21% of the Yankees' payroll.

TRIVIA

The only notable team statistic for both teams was stolen bases.

The Philadelphia Phillies only had the thirteenth-highest payroll
in baseball, but managed to reach the pinnacle anyway.

Not a single one of the twenty-eight highest-paid baseball
players were members of either World Series roster.

2008 WORLD SERIES ROSTER TRIVIA

*Fifty-one players were on the active rosters during the 2008 Fall
Classic. Here's where most of these fifty-one originated:*

28% were born outside of the continental United States.
24% were from California and 10% were born in Illinois.

Overall, nine different countries (plus the territory of Puerto Rico)
were represented in this World Series. Australia, Canada, and
Germany were even on this list.

The Dominican Republic placed the most exports with three, and Japan produced one player for each of the two teams.

Two players came from the state of Rhode Island.

Even the state of Hawaii was represented, but somehow the populous state of New York failed to produce any.

Of these fifty-one World Series athletes:

76% went through the amateur draft, 57% played college baseball, 31% were still with their original franchise, 10% were still in their rookie seasons, and 14% of them had at least ten years of major league experience.

WHAT'S WITH THOSE CRAZY SUITS?
(A drunken screed by Yellowstone Ritter)

More than a few television executives were sad to see the
Phillies and Rays make it into the 2008 World Series.
It's not that they dislike either ball club, it's just that they always
hope for matchups between two HUGE market teams.
From their perspective, a Yankee-Dodger series is the Holy Grail.
To the suits,
the bottom line is more in line with how many hot dogs, apple pies,
and Chevrolets they can help sell.
In a similar fashion, the national media also seems to prefer
the teams that play in their own backyard.
This also makes perfect sense.
After all, these are the clubs and personalities they are
the most familiar with.
But for me and a few zillion other fans, the Phillies-Rays matchup
held just as much dramatic intrigue
and excitement as any
World Series between two big-market teams could have.
No, it wasn't a classic David vs Goliath scenario.

(It was more like a David versus David's little brother.)
But in a few ways, this World Series was even sweeter.
After all,
the Philly victory unified a city in ways that
no Angel, Dodger, Met, or Yankee championship ever could.
In addition, tons of baseball fans in Florida's Bay Area
came together in unprecedented force.
A lot of them even had the class to leave their NY Yankee caps out of
public sight for the entire month of October.
You don't always get that same electricity in a huge market!
I distinctly recall when the Chicago White Sox
won it all back in 2005.
It was a great victory for a great city,
but I noticed that only half of Chicago seemed jubilant.
On the night that the White Sox locked it all up,
the North side of Chitown
wasn't toasting champagne so much as they were,
if anything, mildly depressed by the news.
I guess for Cubs fans, it felt similar to finding out that
their neighbor had won the lottery.
There's another thing about the relatively smaller baseball markets.
When their teams start to gel into championship form,
you begin seeing the team's colors everywhere in public.
Practically one out of five people start to rabidly follow the beat.
However, in the great metropolitan areas like
Chicago, Los Angeles, and New York
(although each area has a tremendous core of fans)
the ratio of fanaticism is relatively sparse.
Maybe only one in twenty people gets the fever.
As for Rollie Fingers,
he loves ALL World Series games no matter who is playing,
but if the A's, Padres, or Brewers are involved,
then that's just a huge bonus for him.
As for my own favorites, it's the strangest thing, but I damn near like
all thirty teams equally.
However, I must give out full disclosure: I've been told by friends

*that I tend to subconsciously root for the teams whose parks
have the best barbecue stands.*

They might have a point.

*However, I'm not so sure that the television executives who crave
NY-LA matchups have a point nearly as sharp.*

*I believe that high baseball ratings are drawn as the direct result of
having drama, excitement, and larger-than-life characters involved
and I think I can prove it.*

*After all, the 2004 World Series drew far better ratings
than the one in 2007
(about 49% better)
despite the fact that the Boston Red Sox played in both.*

*Was the vast differential in viewers because the St. Louis area has a
few more people (about 14% more) living there than the
Denver area has?*

*I don't think so and neither does this half-empty bottle
of bourbon sitting on my desk.*

*I believe it was because the Red Sox in '04 were likable underdogs
with tremendous momentum that greatly appealed to even the most
casual of fans (i.e., my wife).*

*Also, let's not underestimate the gripping drama that Curt Schilling
and his bloody sock provided.*

*Of course, it's understandable that many executives continue to
dream of capturing optimum ratings
by hoping for LA and NY teams to meet in the Fall Classic.*

*After all, it's true that the three Yankees-Dodgers matchups
from 1977, 1978, and 1981 all drew monster numbers.*

*But I, for one, think it was because of the personalities involved far
more than it was the cities involved.*

*After all, each of the following personalities
from those historic matchups
brought either a charisma or intensity that could leap
right through a television screen:*

*Steve Garvey, Goose Gossage, Ron Guidry,
Catfish Hunter, Reggie Jackson,
Tommy Lasorda, Billy Martin, Thurman Munson,*

Reggie Smith, Don Sutton,
Fernando Valenzuela, and Bob Welch.
All of them were solid drawing cards
whether they were trying to be or not.
I suppose somewhere along the line,
the suits assumed the ratings were so high more because of the cities
instead of all the interesting players
and the drama that surrounded them.
I could be wrong (and I am once every five years or so)
but I think if those guys had
been playing each other as members of the
Kansas City Royals against the Philadelphia Phillies,
that the ratings would have been just as high.
After all, wait for it, the highest rating a World Series
ever scored happened in 1980, and it pitted the
Kansas City Royals against the Philadelphia Phillies.
But no one should be surprised by this.
These were very interesting teams with players the fans could
emotionally connect with, to say little about all the
marquee matchups the Series provided.
George Brett, Steve Carlton, Dennis Leonard,
Garry Maddox, Tug McGraw, Amos Otis, Dan Quisenberry,
Pete Rose, Mike Schmidt, and Willie Wilson were
all there for the fireworks.
When it comes to ratings, cities don't matter,
but drama and charisma do.

That's my screed.

9

THE JAPANESE FACTOR

◇◇

I n 2008, MLB had eighteen players who got there by way of the Japanese leagues, four more athletes than in 2007. Ten were pitchers whereas eight were position players.

Many people would be interested to know how these eighteen players did during their rookie American seasons as compared to their final seasons back home in the Orient.

As it turns out, eight of the ten Japanese pitchers saw their ERA go on the rise. Overall, the average pitcher saw his ERA balloon by 2.29 earned runs. Even All-Star Hideki Okajima of the Red Sox nudged his ERA up by 0.08.

As for notching strikeouts, that feat also became more difficult, but not by much. The average Japanese pitcher posted 1.2 fewer strikeouts over the course of the season. However, this aggregate total was affected by the amazing rookie year of Hideo Nomo, who went from 126K in Japan to posting 236 for the Dodgers.

As for the six active pitchers in 2008 who have already played into their sophomore seasons, their ERAs went up another 0.87 and their strikeout totals decreased by an aggregate total of 130 (for an 18% decrease).

However, these numbers need to be taken with a grain of salt. One freshman pitcher, in limited time, posted a whopping 20.25 ERA, and a sophomore pitcher turned in a 13.50 ERA.

So, overall, without these two extreme examples included, we can assert that the typical freshman saw their ERA increase by 0.74 whereas the more acclimated sophomore pitchers saw a decrease in their ERA of 0.41.

There are factors that should play a part in second-season improvement. For some, the degree of homesickness would dissipate. For others, the cultural and language barriers should weaken considerably. Of course, gaining familiarity with their multiple opponents could also help explain improvement, though that notion works both ways.

When comparing how Japanese hitters performed after venturing over to the Western Hemisphere, we found a similar negative effect.

On average, the eight freshman hitters saw their batting averages sink 17 points. Even the phenomenal Ichiro Suzuki went from .387 all the way down to .350 upon crossing the ocean.

But the power totals for these hitters suffered an even more significant dent. During their final seasons in Japan, the octet slugged an aggregate 196 homers, but in America their combined total sank all the way down to 81 (a 59% decrease).

Was there a bounce-back in hitting prowess during their sophomore seasons in America?

Not so much. For the seven active players who have already played a sophomore season, their BA decreased by another 27 points. However, as a group, they did hit 12 more homers, a power increase of 17%.

However, the preceding batting average statistics are somewhat misleading because of a wild anomaly.

So Taguchi, in limited playing time, hit .400 during his initial season in the United States. Although it's hardly so-so that So managed to go 6 for 15 right out of the gate, it doesn't qualify as the standard of a full season of play.

So, by tossing out So's example, we have instead found that the typical Japanese hitter saw his batting average decline 36 points during his initial year in America. As for their sophomore effort, they saw an additional 8-point decrease in their BA.

So, why do some Japanese stars have more success in America than their counterparts? More than likely, it's due to a variety of factors.

First and foremost, some just have a particular skill set that matches up better in Major League Baseball. Two players in Japan with comparable statistics, for example, might fail or succeed in America because one possesses superior velocity or bat speed and therefore isn't overmatched nearly as often as his countryman.

Another factor in success is how well an individual can scout dozens of new opponents (sometimes without the aid of a translator). Being able to adapt quickly will help a newcomer succeed in year one.

Others might conject that the average Japanese "rookie" is either in his prime or on his way down—thus carrying more physical wear and tear than the typical American rook.

Oddly enough, the relative lack of decent Japanese food can also be a detriment. Having to maintain perfect athletic shape outside of your optimum routines and cuisines would be difficult for anyone. In addition, American food tends to be a lot less healthy.

Although it would be politically incorrect to say so, still others would mention that the average player in MLB is superior to the average player in the NPB (Nippon Professional Baseball).

They might point to how MLB draws from a much larger talent pool, and they could also point to the various American exports who tore it up in Japan after getting overmatched in MLB.

But there are also those who disagree with the notion that there is simply more talent in MLB. They point to Japan's success in international competition and also mention that Japanese players have made it into the All-Star Game.

The truth might be somewhere in the middle. The best nine NPB players might be competitive with the best nine MLB players, but it's unclear whether the top ninety players from each league would match up anywhere near as well.

But overall, the playing fields across the two nations is leveling more and more with the passage of time. Athletes such as Ichiro Suzuki and Hideki Okajima have proven this trend. But, on average, jumping the Pacific has proven to be a solid way to say *sayonara* to superior statistics.

10

TEN MAPLE BATS

◇◇◇

On a beautiful spring day in Montana in 2008, not far from the Canadian border, twenty-six-year-old minor leaguer John Odom sat quietly in his motel room. He was miles away from family members and teammates alike. Though every new day brought a chime of hope, each sunset brought yet another chord of disappointment. This wasn't how it was supposed to be.

A few hundred miles to the east, Jared Greenberg and Dan Zimmer were rolling across the wide-open highways of North Dakota. They were in good spirits after a positive business trip in Minneapolis. Their thoughts often drifted to their unique entrepreneurial venture back home in Red Deer, Alberta.

Upward in Calgary, Peter Young, the president of the minor league Vipers, began to brainstorm. Earlier that year, Young had signed John Odom as a free agent. However, the Canadian authorities had stopped his promising new pitcher at the border as there had been a minor blip on his record (dating back nearly ten years). Initally, it seemed trivial, but with each day, the red tape tangled into an even bigger knot.

Earlier that year, Odom had been in spring training with the San Francisco Giants. But surrendering one gopher ball too many had all but packed his suitcase for him and led him to this pastoral limbo. Despite the natural beauty surrounding him, he wanted to be elsewhere. One might say that the sweet grass of rural America can't always replace the even sweeter grass of the baseball diamond.

Jared Greenberg and Dan Zimmer continued their steady drive through dusty parts unknown. The duo was blissfully unaware that their fifteen minutes of fame was circling overhead.

Seven years earlier, with little more than a hand lathe and a few cords of rock maple, they had started up a bat-making company by the name of *Prairie Sticks*. Although they were sending out a lot fewer bats than either Louisville Slugger or Carlsbad Caverns, their customers were satisfied and their work was fulfilling.

Back at the Viper executive office, Peter Young knew he had to cut bait on John Odom because of his legal status. He had contacted a club down in the USA (the Laredo Broncos) and dangled the promising Odom. Peter was hopeful that he could pry away their best hitter, but the talks stalled.

The Broncos countered with cash. Peter refused.

But inspiration struck.

Peter recalled the time that he had tried to move 1,500 old stadium seats in exchange for an opposing player. Hmmm…bartering for him could not only be the ticket, but it might prove to be fun as well. He began to think about what inanimate objects he might accept in exchange for Odom.

Getting traded is part of baseball. All too often, players must pack their bags and head to a new organization. Many times the player isn't happy about getting relocated, but the sting of getting swapped is often lessened when he finds out just how much value his old team received in return.

On May 23, 2008, John Odom got traded from the Vipers to the Broncos for "10 Prairie Sticks double-dipped maple bats, black."

I'm guessing he didn't exactly order pancakes when he found out the news.

Just as it had numerous times before, an order beeped in on voice-mail for Dan and Jared to fill. On average, they had been cutting about thirty bats per week so adding another ten wouldn't be a problem.

But then, something most unusual happened. News of this odd trade hit a kitschy nerve, and national outlets like CNN and ESPN reported it. Orders for maple bats began pouring in to Jared and Dan.

Suddenly, their wood-based company caught fire—but in a good way.

As for Odom, he only ended up pitching three games for Laredo but more than earned the respect of his teammates who knew that his talents were worth a lot more than $655 of equipment.

As for those ten maple bats, well, they never even got used. Ever with an eye for publicity, Peter Young instead sold them for $10,000 to the people at Ripley's. Believe it or not.

Follies Factoids

In 1905, Honus Wagner became the first base-ball player in history to receive endorsement money. The product he put his name on? A signature Louisville Slugger.

Legendary hitter Ted Williams made it an annual ritual to travel to Kentucky. Once there, he would spend hours meticulously going through piles and piles of wood. Only when he found the right specimen could his customized Louisville Sluggers be processed.

Although carved knobs began appearing on the ends of bats as early as 1879, Babe Ruth made history in 1919 by becoming the first known player to order bats with knobs on them. Babe hit 29 homers that year, up from 11 the year before. The following year, the Bambino blasted 54 homers. No other player in 1920 had as many as 19. Was his power display all because of these customized bats? Probably not...but they sure didn't hurt the cause.

11

BUCKY DENT REVISITED AGAIN

◇◇

It's nearly unfathomable that the great Boston teams of the 1970s didn't win a single world championship.

Year in and year out, they posted winning records and did lots of damage to lots of other ball clubs. I should know. They were the ones that swept my Oakland A's in the '75 ALCS—effectively ending our run as kings of the mountain.

But among these many powerhouse Red Sox teams, I'd argue that they were at their absolute pinnacle in '78. Quite possibly, this may have been the best team in history to never win it all.

The 1978 Red Sox were so good that they placed four outfielders on the All-Star team. They were so good their number nine hitter (Dwight Evans) clocked 24 homers. They were so good their closer (Bob Stanley) went 15-2.

But as every Boston Red Sox fan worth their salt knows, things went bad for them…heartbreakingly bad.

Which reminds me, if you ever want to have a little fun, walk into any pub in Boston, get everyone's attention, and then, loud and proud, say the following words in your best "announcer" voice:

Deep to left!! Yastrzemski will NOT get it!
It's a HOME RUN!!!
A 3-run home run for BUCKY DENT!!!!! And the Yankees now lead it by a score of 3–2.

Within seconds, you'll be the recipient of a lot of free beer—some of which will even be in bottles.

The legend of Bucky Dent's improbable home run over the Green Monster is indelible in the minds of Red Sox and Yankee fans alike.

Let me recap:

In mid-July of 1978, Boston held a massive fourteen-game lead on the Yanks. But by mid-September, New York had not only erased the deficit, they had moved ahead to secure a three-and-a-half game lead.

From that point on, the Red Sox snapped into high gear. They won twelve out of the last fourteen games, and the two clubs finished the regular season with identical 99–63 records. This tie forced an extra game to be played that wasn't on the original schedule.

When all was said and done, the Yankees prevailed, in large part due to a 3-run homer at the hands of a shortstop who entered the game with a humble .309 slugging permillage.

Bucky Dent became an instant Yankee legend. But, ironically, it was the Boston fans who would christen him with a new nickname—one that has lasted through the decades. I can't type that nickname here, but I can tell you that it sounds a bit like Bucky Truckin' Dent.

To Red Sox fans, Dent became the latest symbol of their perpetually dashed dreams. He was the exact opposite of a scapegoat. He was, in essence, a scapedent.

But what few know is that there was another player at Fenway Park the day before who may have done EVEN MORE than Bucky to dent Boston's chances of reaching the post that year.

The following is that player's story……….

12

THE SPOILER

◇◇

I n 1978, the Toronto Blue Jays had a rookie centerfielder by the name of Rick Bosetti. On the field, he was known both for his speed and for his knack for cutting down greedy baserunners.

But off the field, his teammates recognized his true calling—he was an ingenious practical joker. Bosetti was capable of stunts so hysterically cruel that it was no wonder the Jays were his third organization in as many seasons.

Toronto was the cellar dweller in 1978, but that's an understatement. Truth be told, they had pretty much fallen out of contention by Arbor Day. By the time mid-September rolled around, they were thirty-three-and-a-half games out of first place.

But the Bluebirds' hopes weren't entirely dashed. Why? The schedule had placed them in the enviable position of spoiler. Six of their final twelve games would be against the first-place Yankees while the other six would be against the second-place Red Sox. Every Toronto game would have huge significance.

The Yankees were first to visit Toronto's Exhibition Stadium, and they sent Ron Guidry to the mound. "Gator" entered this game with twenty-two wins against only two losses, which was a tad intimidating, given that the Blue Jays' win leader had only ten victories.

It was Rick Bosetti's job to lead off against the man who would

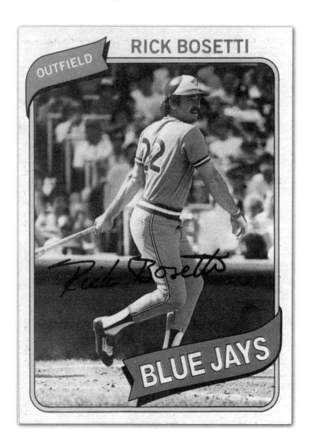

eventually win the Cy Young Award that year. To most every fan in the stadium, it was a serious mismatch.

However, Bosetti never got the memo. He lined a single to left field to open the game. A hit parade began and Bosetti scored the game's first run. The Yankee armor had officially been chinked.

In the second inning, Bosetti faced off against Louisiana Lighting again, but this time the results were different.

He hit a triple. In fact, Guidry never made it out of that inning, and the Blue Jays went on to defeat the Yankees 8–1. The Red Sox were very pleased.

However, Toronto ended up dropping the final two games of the series to the Bronx Bombers. Even so, they still had their swagger because Boston was coming into town, and they were aching to do as much damage as possible.

That first game with the Red Sox was nip and tuck. Neither team could put the contest out of reach. The game headed into the bottom of the ninth inning with Boston leading 4–3.

The tension in the stadium was so thick, you could have cut it with a cliché. Bob Bailor opened with a single for the hometown birds, but the subsequent hitter's attempt to move him over failed when the bunt was caught in mid-air. Doh!

With one out and the tying run at first, Dave McKay singled, sending Bailor to third. That made things a tad more interesting. Pinch hitter Doug Ault then came to the plate and patiently worked a walk to load the bases. It was at that point that things got a lot more interesting.

The fans tilted forward to the edge of their seats.

At this point, All-Star Bill Campbell was summoned from the bullpen. The first hitter Soup had to face? Rick Bosetti.

Campbell stared in. Bosetti stared out. The next pitch could conceivably end the game in victory for either team.

Soup hurled the ball and Bosetti smoked a single that brought home both Bailor and McKay. The Canadian crowd erupted with joy at the thrilling end to the game, but it was the faraway Yankees who were even happier. With only eight games remaining in the season, thanks to Bosetti, the Red Sox had fallen back by two full games.

But during the next contest, Boston rebounded and handed Toronto a loss—a victory that coincided with a Yankee loss.

New England breathed out a collective sigh of relief. With only seven games to play, only one game separated the two hated archrivals.

What happened next was unprecedented.

Boston won their next five games. However, the first-place Yankees also won their next five. The Red Sox were basically playing perfect baseball but couldn't catch a break.

As for the Blue Jays, their plans on becoming spoilers were being spoiled, and the immediate future wasn't looking that much brighter with only two games remaining.

On the Saturday of the final weekend of the regular season, the Jays found themselves at beautiful Fenway Park. However, they had the misfortune of drawing eventual Hall of Famer Dennis Eckersley, who was an ace at that point of his career.

Setting the tone for the entire game, Eck struck out the side in the first inning. After that—he settled down.

In the bottom of the first inning, the Red Sox patched together 4 runs. The game was practically over before it had even begun.

But, early in the game, something strange happened. A loud chorus of boos rang through Fenway Park for no apparent reason. Rick Bosetti looked around the field and even up into the stands but saw nothing unusual. He wondered what had caused the Fenway Faithful to come so completely unglued.

Finally, Bosetti saw it.

The old-time manual scoreboard that sits at the base of the Green Monster in left-center showed that the distant Yankees had racked up a five-run lead. Bosetti didn't know it at the time, but the acorn of an idea had been planted.

Like clockwork, the Red Sox finished off the Jays that day. But like additional clockwork, the Yankees vanquished their opponents as well. Only one game remained in the season.

The tension throughout Boston was near a breaking point.

This had become so much more than just a simple divisional race. This was personal, especially because the Yanks were the defending World Series champions and were perceived as arrogant by the Red Sox nation. As for Boston, well, they were absolutely starving for a World Series championship, especially since they hadn't won it all since the days when Woodrow Wilson was in the White House.

On a religious Sunday morning in early October, Boston fans, with fingers crossed, made their way into the ball park.

With baited breath, they were hoping for just two little miracles—a Boston win AND a Yankee loss. Any other scenario would eliminate them. On that day, Fenway Park became a church and sent out more prayers than all the other New England houses of worship combined.

Meanwhile, the Yankees were in their element, getting ready to host the Cleveland Indians. They were pitching the legendary Catfish Hunter whereas the Tribe was offering up Rick Waits—a good pitcher, but one who came attached to a losing record. You could say that a lot of Yankee fans began making early playoff plans.

Up in Boston, all the Red Sox went into their pregame rituals, but they worked out with a focus that was even more impressive than usual. The Blue Jays, however, were relatively relaxed, but even so, their goals were clearly defined. They wanted to not only beat the Red Sox, but to do so *before* the Yankees could manage to put away Cleveland. That way, they could have the pride in knowing that they had been the eliminators.

As the Blue Jays took infield practice, Rick Bosetti wandered out toward left-center. The historic scoreboard at the base of the Green Monster caught his eye. It was then that it happened; his acorn of an idea from the day before sprouted into a full-grown oak.

13

THE SPOILER, PART II: INFILTRATING THE GREEN MONSTER

◇◇◇

The Green Monster is the most unusual outfield fence in all of baseball. Fans mostly think of it as a colorful wall that is over thirty-seven feet high. Pitchers, however, think of it as the closest left-field porch in all of baseball.

To see it on television is nice. To see it from the grandstand is beautiful. To see it from the pitcher's mound is terrifying. A key to pitching well at Fenway is to never turn around to look at the wall. As it is with most green monsters (like Godzilla and Frankenstein), it's best to avoid eye contact.

But Rick Bosetti was an outfielder, so he had no such aversion. His eyes scanned the soft underbelly of the Green Monster until he found the door at its base. In short order, he inquisitively approached it. Like so many other young players, he was compelled to see just what was behind the green door.

TAP TAP TAP

There was no response.

TAP TAP TAP TAP

Finally, a young ballpark employee answered the door with a surprised look on his face

"Can I help you?"

Bosetti disarmingly countered with a "Hi, I was just wondering if

I could check out where you work?"

This was an unusual request. They both knew it. But despite his confusion, the employee ushered the ballplayer inside to give him a quick look-see. Like a schoolboy on a field trip, Bosetti began to ask the scoreboard operator all sorts of questions about how the job worked.

It was explained how the various scores going on all across the country would get relayed to the park via shortwave radio. At that point, the listener would call the scoreboard operator by telephone to give him the key information.

Then, the rectangular metal plates with the numerals on them would be slid into proper position so that the thousands of fans in attendance could stay properly informed.

Fenway Park was packed to the rafters. The familiar hum of over 30,000 people started to rise in pitch. The game was only ten minutes away from starting so Bosetti knew he had to act fast.

With all the charm he could muster, Bosetti asked the young employee if he could play a harmless little joke. Not being in the habit of ever saying no to a ballplayer, the young operator indifferently granted Bosetti carte blanche to the scoreboard.

Locating the corresponding slots, Bosetti found a "zero" and slid it into the slot next to the plate already marked "CLE."

He then took a "5" plate and slid it directly across from the "NYY" plate.

Voila!

Immediately, a thunderous boo sliced through the Fenway crowd. Struggling to keep his laughing jag under control, Bosetti then slid the "F" plate into position. With this move, the loud commotion in the stands had the life sucked out of it.

The crowd was aghast. Within Bosetti's phantom game, the Yankees hadn't only beaten the Indians by 5 runs, they had wrapped the whole game up. His deed hadn't gone unnoticed inside the Red Sox dugout. Many of Don Zimmer's players and coaches just stared at the scoreboard as though there had to be some colossal mistake. As pain and disappointment began to course throughout Red Sox nation, others became skeptical. After all, how could it be that the Indian-Yankee game could be over so early in the day?

But ripples of damage had already been done, for the thought of a Yankee victory was so thoroughly sickening to the New Englanders.

Shortly thereafter, the scoreboard was made honest. All the Red Sox fans and players let go a sigh of relief, but perhaps some permanent psychological damage had been done.

Once both games were underway, the scoreboard operators in both Boston and the Bronx became more important than usual.

The Indians opened the first inning by scoring 2 runs. This drew some applause from the Boston crowd, but not as much as you might think. After all, some may have grown jaded.

This was justified, as in the bottom of the frame, the Yankees matched with a pair of runs off of Rick Waits. Just about everyone in New England began to wonder just when this roller coaster would stop.

But it was in the top of the second inning that Christmas came early. The Indians scored 4 runs. As though he was dispensing a life-saving vaccine, the Fenway Park scoreboard operator slid that magical "4" plate into place and the crowd began to cheer.

On the field, Luis Tiant was mowing down the Jays. He was in the midst of retiring the first eleven hitters, but unfortunately for him, the bats of his teammates were being silenced as well.

But in the bottom of the fifth inning, the Red Sox broke through to stake Tiant to a 2-run lead. For good measure, down in the Bronx, the Indians padded another run to their lead as well.

When all was said and done, the Tribe's Rick Waits wrapped up a 5-hit, complete-game victory against New York at Yankee Stadium. A few minutes later, 206 miles away, Luis Tiant wrapped up his own masterpiece, a 2-hit shutout.

Oddly enough, Rick Bosetti's fictional 5–0 score proved to be prescient, but instead it was the Red Sox on the winning end of that score and not the Yankees.

These two games set the stage for the Bucky Dent game to be played the next day.

Would the outcome of that makeshift "sudden death" game had been different if the Red Sox hadn't been victims of Bosetti's practical joke?

Furthermore, would they have been able to win the division by one game if a certain center fielder from Toronto hadn't hit a walk-off single against them earlier that month?

Who knows? But it sure makes you wonder.

Follies Factoids

From 1978 to 2008, the Boston Red Sox finished in second place more often than any other team (twelve times).

The silver medal for winning the most silver medals goes to the New York Mets, who, from 1978 to 2008, finished in second place eleven times.

14

THE
JIM RICE
DOSSIER

RICE, Jim

DOSSIER - 14

EARLY CHILDHOOD: Anderson, South Carolina

BOYHOOD DREAM: To become a professional basketball player

DRAFTED: Was the 15th pick in the 1971 June draft

PROS DRAFTED AHEAD OF HIM INCLUDED:
Danny Goodwin, Frank Tanana, and Tom Veryzer

MINOR LEAGUE GAMES: 436

MOST FREQUENT MINOR LEAGUE HOME: Winter Haven, Florida

MINOR LEAGUE ACCOMPLISHMENTS:
In 1974, Rice won the Class AAA Triple Crown
Led Pawtucket to a Junior World Series victory

DEBUT YEAR: 1974 (as a late-season call up)

AGE AT DEBUT: 21

ROOKIE YEAR (1975) ACCOMPLISHMENTS:
Key player in Boston winning the AL pennant
Finished third in the AL MVP voting
Finished second in the AL Rookie-of-the-Year voting

RICE, Jim

EARLIEST TEAMMATES INCLUDED: Carl Yastrzemski, Carlton Fisk, Bill "Spaceman" Lee, Juan Marichal, Dwight Evans

EARLY NICKNAME: Teammate Fred Lynn and Rice were once known as "The Gold Dust Twins"

FINAL SEASON: 1989

FINAL TEAMMATES INCLUDED: Wade Boggs, Roger Clemens, Lee Smith, Oil Can Boyd, and Dwight Evans

PRIMARY MANAGER: Don Zimmer

TOTAL MANAGERS PLAYED FOR: 6

TOTAL SEASONS IN THE MAJOR LEAGUES: 16

NUMBER OF LOSING SEASONS: 2

CAREER STATS:
.298 BA/382 HR/1,451 RBI

REGULAR SEASON WINNING PERCENTAGE IN GAMES IN WHICH RICE PARTICIPATED: 54%

RICE, Jim

MAJOR LEAGUE AFFILIATIONS:
Boston Red Sox (100%)

POSITIONS PLAYED (rounded):

LF	72%	PH	1%
DH	26%	CF	1 game
RF	2%		

INJURY AND/OR REST RATE: 11%

BEST SEASON: (1978) .315 BA/46 HR/139 RBI

MOST FREQUENT FOE:
Jim Slaton - 96 plate appearances (.233 BA/1 HR/7 RBI)

THE PITCHER HE HOMERED MOST OFTEN AGAINST:
Jim Palmer (9)

THE PITCHER HE OWNED:
Dennis Martinez: .376 (32 for 85) with 7 HRs, 26 RBIs, 7 walks, and 8 strikeouts.

THE PITCHER WHO OWNED HIM:
Danny Darwin: .109 (5 for 46) with 0 HRs, 3 RBIs, 2 walks, and 10 strikeouts.

THE PITCHER HE STRUCK OUT MOST OFTEN AGAINST:
Jim Palmer (24)

RICE, Jim

DOSSIER - 14

HIS RECORD AGAINST HALL OF FAME PITCHERS:
429 AT-BATS (.247 BA/24 HR/70 RBI/116K)

LEAGUE HOME RUN CHAMPION: 3 times

LEAGUE MVP: 1 time

MOST FREQUENT OPPONENT: Cleveland Indians

HOME AWAY FROM HOME:
Yankee Stadium (.336 BA/22 HR/66 RBI)

ALL-STAR TEAMS: 8

ALL-STAR STATS:
20 AT-BATS: .200 BA/1 HR/1 RBI

PLAYOFF RECORD:
2 postseasons — 18 games
71 AT-BATS: .225 BA/2 HR/7 RBI
1 pennant   0 world championships

CLOSEST STATISTICAL TWIN: Orlando Cepeda

HALL OF FAME CALIBRE RATING: 115%

RICE, Jim

MISC. NOTES: In 1975, during the last week of the regular season, Rice's hand was broken on a pitch, shelving him for the year prematurely. However, after Rice watched the Red Sox take out Oakland in the ALCS, he cut off his cast and proclaimed himself ready to play against the Cincinnati Reds in the World Series.

Red Sox brass felt otherwise and fearing long-term damage, kept him on the disabled list.

The Red Sox went on to lose in seven games.

Eleven years later, Rice made it back to the World Series, but this time he was more than ready for duty. Against the New York Mets, he went 9 for 27, but once again, the Red Sox lost the seventh game and went home broken-hearted.

* * *

Once in Yankee Stadium, a fan reached over the railing and snatched away his ball cap. Reacting quickly, Rice leapt the railing and went up into enemy territory after it.

* * *

Bill James once reported that he saw Jim Rice break his bat on a checked swing.

* * *

In 1982, a teammate lined a baseball into the stands that severely injured a four-year-old boy. Rice immediately rushed into the crowd, snatched up the victim, and carried the severely bleeding tyke into the clubhouse to receive expert medical treatment. Many speculate that this was the first time in history that someone saving another person's life was broadcast on live television.

A FOLLIES TRIVIA QUIZ

Question 1: What do George Washington, Babe Ruth, Sparky Anderson, Tom Seaver, and Ken Griffey Jr. all have in common?

Question 2: Four hurlers managed to save at least one hundred games during both the 1970s and 1980s. Name these four closers. *Hint*: Three of these four are enshrined in Cooperstown.

Question 3: In the first baseball game ever televised, who was the first hitter to come up to the plate?

Answers on page 95.

15

THE EVOLUTION OF THE SLUGGER

SELECTED HOME RUN CHAMPIONS THROUGH HISTORY
(1908 – 2008)

1908   *Tim Jordan* of the seventh-place Dodgers led all of base-ball with <u>12</u> home runs.

1918   *Babe Ruth* of the World Series champion Red Sox tied with *Tilly Walker* of the last-place Athletics with <u>11</u> home runs apiece.

1928   Babe Ruth of the World Series champion Yankees led with <u>54</u> home runs.

1938   *Hank Greenberg* of the fourth-place Tigers led with <u>58</u> home runs.

1948   *Ralph Kiner* of the fourth-place Pirates tied with Johnny Mize of the fifth-place Giants with <u>40</u> home runs apiece.

1958   *Ernie Banks* of the fifth-place Cubs led with <u>47</u> home runs.

1968   *Frank Howard* of the last-place Senators led with <u>44</u> home runs.

1978   *Jim Rice* of the second-place Red Sox led with <u>46</u> home runs.

1988   *Jose Canseco* of the pennant-winning A's led with <u>42</u> home runs.

1998   *Mark McGwire* of the third-place Cardinals led with <u>70</u> home runs.

2008   *Ryan Howard* of the World Champion Phillies led with <u>48</u> home runs.

ON AVERAGE, HOW OFTEN DID THESE SLUGGERS WALK?

Tim Jordan ~ every 2.5 games
"1918" Babe Ruth ~ every 1.6 games
Tilly Walker ~ every 2.8 games
"1928" Babe Ruth ~ every 1.1 games
Hank Greenberg ~ every 1.3 games
Ralph Kiner ~ every 1.4 games
Johnny Mize ~ every 1.6 games
Ernie Banks ~ every 3.0 games
Frank Howard ~ every 2.9 games
Jim Rice ~ every 2.8 games
Jose Canseco ~ every 2.0 games
Mark McGwire ~ every 0.96 games
Ryan Howard ~ every 0.5 games

SLUGGIN'
ERNIE
BANKS
"MR. CUB"

ON AVERAGE, HOW OFTEN DID THESE SLUGGERS STRIKE OUT?

Tim Jordan ~ data not available
"1918" Babe Ruth ~ every 1.6 games
Tilly Walker ~ every 2.6 games
"1928" Babe Ruth ~ every 1.8 games
Hank Greenberg ~ every 1.7 games ⟍
Ralph Kiner ~ every 2.6 games
Johnny Mize ~ every 4.1 games
Ernie Banks ~ every 1.8 games
Frank Howard ~ every 1.1 games ✗
Jim Rice ~ every 1.3 games
Jose Canseco ~ every 1.2 games
Mark McGwire ~ every 1.0 games
Ryan Howard ~ every 1.2 games

Various conclusions can be drawn from this data. Obviously having the biggest slugger in the league doesn't mean you'll have a good team. Of course, it doesn't hurt, but even though fans have revered the home run hitter since the Babe first started belting them over the fence, a winning team needs much more to succeed.

To me, the trend that sticks out in this breakdown is how the only home run champions in the batch to win World Series rings (Babe Ruth and Ryan Howard) managed to work an especially high number of walks.

Follies Factoids

The 2000 season was not only the most prolific year for home runs in baseball history (5,693 were hit in the 2,429 regular season games played), but it was the season in which there were more home runs per game (2.34) than during any other baseball season.

16

MIKE HARGROVE AND LOU PINIELLA: A SHARED LIFE

◇◇

A look at the many similarities between two baseball icons.

Both were born in the 1940s.

Both grew up in the South.

Both played high school basketball.

Both played college baseball.

Both made their major league debuts within three years
of being drafted.

Both were American League Rookies of the Year.

Both played in the AL from 1974 to 1984.

Both spent significant time in left field, at first base,
and as designated hitters.

Both wore the uniform of the Cleveland Indians.

Both wore the uniform of the Baltimore Orioles.

Both wore the uniform of the Seattle Mariners.

Both were teammates of Bobby Bonds.

Both were teammates of Toby Harrah.

Both played for manager Billy Martin.

Both hit in excess of .300 six times,
but neither ended up a lifetime .300 hitter.

Both surpassed the 1,600-hit barrier.

Both were selected to participate in an All-Star Game.

Both went 0 for 1 in their lone at-bat in the Midsummer Classic.

Both went on to become even more successful as managers.

Both returned to the All-Star Game as managers.

Both skippers made it to the postseason on at least five occasions.

Both had a vice-president by the name of Johnson.
(Scratch that—wrong list)

Both sat out an entire season in between managerial jobs.

Both managed Ichiro Suzuki.

Both managers won pennants with teams from Ohio.

Both Hargrove and Piniella managed in excess of two thousand
games.

Both possess winning records as managers.

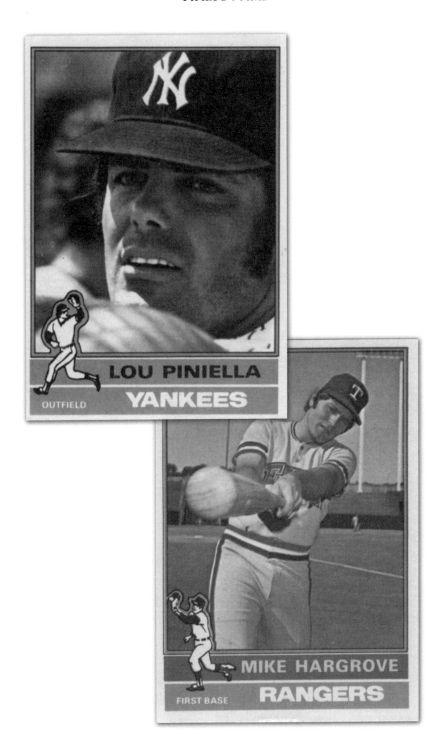

17

THE (PURCHASING) POWER OF A-ROD AND THE BABE

⬦⬦

RUTHIAN AND RODRIGUEZIAN PROPORTIONS

In 1930, Babe Ruth earned a salary of $75,000. He also took in another forty grand in endorsements. In current dollars, due to inflation, the Babe would have made the equivalent of around $925,000 in salary plus an additional 495K in endorsements.

By comparison, in 2007 Alex Rodriguez earned a whopping $29 million from baseball (base salary plus incentives), and then pocketed an additional $6 million from endorsements. Indexing inflation, in terms of real purchasing power, A-Rod made more than twenty-four times the amount Babe Ruth did.

But of course, since 1930, live attendance is up more than seven-fold and the amount of bucks baseball brings in has exploded due to television contracts and other revenue streams. In addition, the power of the reserve clause has been greatly diminished (thank you, Curt Flood)—so this disparity is to be expected.

There are a lot of unique ways to break down how it is that Alex Rodriguez earns his money. You could say that he makes about $225,000 per game, injured or not, or you could instead break it

THE
BABE
AND
A-ROD

RODRIGUEZ NEW YORK AMER.

Yours Truly "Babe" Ruth

© I-L-P
#6

#6

down as $750,000 per home run. Another way to look at it is that A-Rod made about 65K per at-bat whether he struck out looking or hit a grand slam—good work if you can find it!

What would happen if a player only got paid per at-bat? I imagine we would see a lot fewer walks or sacrifices—which is why no sane general manager would ever sign such a deal. A player in that position would probably hack away at everything. After all, if he walked… whoosh…there goes sixty-five big ones. That would be kind of hard to explain to the wife.

Since it's about forty feet from the on-deck circle to home plate, another way to configure A-Rod's income is to say he makes $1,625 per foot to the plate. If that were the case, the Yankees would save millions by moving the on-deck circle adjacent to the batter's box.

Sure, it might be dangerous to expose this great player to such risks, but I think that it would greatly help attendance, especially at road games in Boston, Texas, and Seattle. If the Steinbrenners are reading this, you're welcome for the great idea, and hey, no hurry, you can always thank me later.

Follies Factoids

Almost every baseball fan knows Barry Bonds (762) broke Hank Aaron's home run record (755), and they also know that Hank Aaron broke Babe Ruth's home run record (714) but few know that the man Babe Ruth surpassed to become the all-time home-run king was Hall of Famer Roger Connor (138).

Amazingly, Alex Rodriguez reached 500 home runs at a younger age than anyone else in history. However, Babe Ruth managed to get there in 115 fewer games than A-Rod.

18

THE WEALTHIEST BASEBALLER OF ALL-TIME

◇◇

There is one baseball player who even Alex Rodriguez might have to admit carries a heavier wallet than he does.

This fact is ironic because many people don't consider this billionaire to have been nearly as much of a success in the major leagues as A-Rod. After all, the guy only played in seven games, chalking up a 16.76 earned run average in the process. But still, he somehow ended up with a net worth that would make most baseball owners envious.

Massachusetts's Matt White was a great high school pitcher. He played so well that he got the nod to play college ball at Clemson. His stuff in South Carolina was good enough that the Cleveland Indians drafted him in 1998.

But after five seasons and 120 games in their minor league system, Matt found himself plucked away by the Boston Red Sox organization in a Rule V draft.

Then along came 2003—the year that would change his life.

In midseason, the Red Sox brought him up to the bigs, where he made his major league debut at Yankee Stadium. That was his good news. The bad news is that the Bombers busted him for 6 runs in two-thirds of an inning.

Welcome to the show, meat.

Less than a week later, he had been shelled twice more in Toronto so he was off the squad before he even had the chance to pitch in Fenway. The rest of the year would prove rocky for him as he ended up bouncing through the systems of the Mariners, Indians, and, of course, the Rockies.

But on a personal level, 2003 was truly groundbreaking for Matt. Since his elderly aunt needed funds to enter a nursing home, he gave her $50,000 of his major league salary in exchange for her old home and for the property surrounding it.

Matt had plans to build a brand new home there from the ground up, but baseball was his top priority. He spent much of the next two years toiling away in Triple A before earning himself a brief cup of coffee with the Washington Nationals. As for his second priority, his property, he began noticing unusual things with the land starting with the fact that it seemed too dense for building a suitable foundation.

In 2006, Matt finally realized what he was sitting on when a surveyor let him know that the fifty acres he purchased was sitting on nearly twenty-four million tons of valuable rock called Goshen stone—a mother lode estimated to be worth nearly $2.5 billion.

How would you like to get that phone call? Matt did.

What did he do when he found out the good news? He did what any true baseball player would do. He kept playing.

By 2007, he had worked his way into a spring training invitation with the Dodgers. He didn't make the cut, but it led to a forty-game stint with their farm club in Las Vegas. He ended the year in Japan playing for the Yokohama Bay Stars.

As for his lesser priority, the rock, Matt has so far made some small-scale extractions on his own to the extent that he's more than covered the cost of the original purchase price. Eventually, he will probably get around to fully mining the possibilities, but it won't likely happen until he's hung up his cleats for good.

After all, a man's got to have his priorities straight.

19

NINETEENTH CENTURY BROOKLYN

◇◇

Brooklyn, that vibrant ninety-six-square-mile chunk of land on the western tip of Long Island, was once sleepy. In 1801, the town only had about six thousand human residents.

They moved about in a semi-forested land that may have been a perfect blend of rural and urban. Both fruit orchards and bakeries were plentiful. The air was pure if not downright sweet.

Paddlewheel ferries, powered by trotting horses that rotated around a crankshaft, sold passage to Manhattan for four cents—but most Brooklynites had little need to ever leave their island for the other.

Bare feet were common, but shoes were commonplace. Vendors at open-air marketplaces sold items such as hot corn, berries, mint, hot yams, and radishes.

Dutch cottages, dusty roads, herds of cattle, and juvenile thievery were all common sights of the day. Everyone from chimney sweeps to milk-men wailed forth their running commentaries to no one in particular.

Few could have predicted that this rustic berg would eventually explode into America's third-largest city. Even fewer could have predicted that the children's game of "stick and ball" would not only end up inciting the interest of adults, but that it would propel Brooklyn into becoming baseball's earliest hotbed.

By 1825, Brooklyn's population had doubled. Additional factories and piers had sprouted up like dandelions. More and more ships moved in and out with great frequency, many of which had actually been built in the city's own shipyards.

Some of the older residents decried the sudden congestion, but many of their grandchildren would grow up to reflect on the era as quaint. More and more trees were coming down so that more and more buildings could go up.

Large sugar refineries cropped up as did breweries. Fields where there had once been forests began to appear—much to the delight of young adults who were now playing more sophisticated versions of their childhood games.

By 1850, Brooklyn had busted wide open and was supporting in excess of 138,000 people. Thousands continued to pour in at such a clip that the population would double again by the decade's end.

Tensions were on the rise. This densely packed melting pot had a serious need to blow off steam. Just as in neighboring Manhattan, numerous amateur baseball clubs had sprouted up, but the contests in Brooklyn were far more likely to be played by men who worked in shipyards than by those who sailed on yachts. Excellent players emerged and were eventually cherry-picked away to play for Brooklyn's semi-professional teams.

In 1855, the Atlantic Base Ball Club came into existence. Although the timeline is not continuous, these ten men, these "Brooklyn Atlantics," zygotically formed what would evolve into today's Dodger franchise.

Within three years of the birth of the Atlantics, the city of Brooklyn was home to eight semi-pro clubs (and seventy-one amateur ones). Neither Manhattan nor Boston nor Philadelphia could come close to matching Brooklyn's prolific numbers in this regard.

The city's favorite outdoor recreational activity was proving to be quite the spectator sport as well. In 1858, for the first time in history, admission was charged to see a baseball game.

Was this history-making contest played in Brooklyn?

The answer is, surprisingly, no. The game was played in the neutral site of Queens, but it did involve Brooklyn's all-stars battling the best players from Manhattan. (In a sense, this event foreshadowed modern times since Queens now hosts Major League Baseball whereas both Brooklyn and Manhattan do not).

In 1859, the first formal championship in history was decided...and the winners were Brooklyn's Atlantic Base Ball Club. They beat fifteen clubs from Manhattan, the Bronx, and of course, Brooklyn for this high honor.

In 1862, the world's first enclosed baseball field (Union Grounds) opened for business and Brooklyn was its home. At the time, ten cents was a lot of dough to fork over to see any form of entertainment, but to those baseball-craving Brooklynites, it was a bargain.

Union Grounds was not only historic, but also utilitarian, for in the winter, the owner flooded it so that the public could use it as an ice-skating rink. Try picturing this happening nowadays at your nearest baseball stadium.

In 1864, the world's second enclosed baseball field opened up and it, too, was in Brooklyn. Baseball fanatics, or fans as they came to be called, supported this venue in droves as well. Right around this time, businessmen began to figure out that serious money could be made at this if it were better organized.

In 1870 a new era for the city began when work commenced on the Brooklyn Bridge, the architectural marvel of its time. A symbol of optimism and progress, the stone and cement towers of the bridge would momentarily become the tallest structures in all of America. By this point, a prolific matrix of railways dotted the terrain, making Brooklyn one of the most frenetic cities in the world. Even though the population was already in excess of 400,000, immigrants continued to flood into the bustling metropolis, and baseball was there to greet them.

In 1871, the first professional baseball league (the National Association) came into existence. Incredibly, none of Brooklyn's semi-pro teams gained entry, but the relatively superb facility of Union Grounds did become home to the New York Mutuals—a ball club with Manhattan origins. However, Brooklyn was represented because many of the city's best ballplayers (such as George Zeitlein and Fred Treacey) departed to play for the various teams of this higher league.

By 1872, in a whirl of poetic justice, the National Association expanded and two Brooklyn teams (the Atlantics and the Eckfords) were among the beneficiaries. However, with their rosters depleted from the previous season's exodus, the two ball clubs were less than spectacular, and the Eckfords folded after just one season.

The entire National Association ended up folding toward the end of 1875. However, six of the league's teams joined the brand new "National League" that formed in 1876—and the New York Mutuals were among them. Some of the other original NL teams were the Boston Red Stockings and the Chicago White Stockings (now better known respectively as the

Atlanta Braves and the Chicago Cubs).

The league constricted in 1877, and the New York Mutuals were one of the casualties. They were canned in part because they failed to go on road trips late in the season in order to save money.

After that expulsion, Brooklyn only hosted independent and minor league baseball for a six-year period, but the fans remained both loyal and rabid. As for the famed Union Grounds, though it was once state of the art, by 1883 it had become old hat and was demolished.

But 1883 also saw the rebirth of the Brooklyn Atlantics (as a minor league team). They played their ball in the city's newest jewel, Washington Park, which was so named because it was built on a historic site where General Washington himself had once headquartered a command.

The ensuing year, riding tremendous momentum, the Brooklyn Atlantics became a major league team. They were part of the brand spanking new American Association, which competed with the National League and triggered a series of mergers and acquisitions.

In 1885, the Atlantics became known as the Grays, which was the name of a minor league team that had shared Washington Park with them.

In 1888, the Grays absorbed the New York Metropolitan baseball club as well. Because so many of their players on this newly conjoined team were on the verge of marriage, the team was renamed the Brooklyn Bridegrooms. I suppose that's a better name than the Brooklyn Bachelors, but not by much.

The year 1890 was an historic one for Brooklyn baseball. Two teams from the declining American Association jumped to the far more powerful National League—and the Brooklyn Bridegrooms were among them. (The Cincinnati Red Stockings were the other.)

Brooklyn was once again represented in the premiere league in baseball.

How did they do?

They finished in first place behind the play of such stalwarts as Oyster Burns, Adonis Terry, Pop Corkhill, Lady Baldwin, and Germany Smith. I like all those names, in part, because they make "Rollie Fingers" seem so normal.

But even with the Bridegrooms the toast of Brooklyn, this city of 800,000 people was also well represented on the lesser fronts.

THE PRIDE OF BROOKLN
WEE WILLIE
KEELER

Base Ball Club

Williamson

Brooklyn

CHAMPIONS OF AMERICA.

Entered according to Act of Congress, in the year 1865, by CHAS. H. WILLIAMSON, in the
Clerk's Office of the District Court of the United States, of the Eastern
District of New York.

A brand new team, the Brooklyn Gladiators, had replaced the Bridegrooms in the American Association.

In addition, a third baseball league popped up (the Players League) and the Brooklyn Ward's Wonders were a part of the action. For the only time in history, baseball had three leagues—and only two cities (Brooklyn and Philadelphia) were represented in all of them.

In 1891 the Players League went out of business after just one year, but the Grooms managed to absorb the Wonders. As for the American Association, they managed to limp along for one final year, but it was without the last-place Brooklyn Gladiators, who had folded after just one season in the sun.

During the 1890s, the Brooklyn franchise hopped around from venue to venue like frogs on a lilly pad. All told, they played their home games at three different fields, including the notorious Eastern Park—infamous for how confusing it was to arrive there on the city's network of street trolleys.

Brooklyn's nicknames changed often as well, with the Grooms reverting back to being known as the Bridegrooms before becoming the Superbas—a nod to a famous acrobatic troupe of the time. But on the street, these official nicknames were often ignored as fans called the team the "Trolley Dodgers."

This slang term served both as a nod to the scrappy jaywalking efficiency of Brooklynites and as a passive-aggressive slap to the more cultured Manhattanites, who preferred the Giants.

In 1899, Brooklyn's team improved dramatically when the owner added to it several key players from his other team, the Baltimore Orioles. As a result, the team became a bona-fide powerhouse with the likes of Wee Willie Keeler and Joe Kelley leading the way.

Brooklyn ended the nineteenth century with two consecutive championships, victories which no doubt reminded the old-timers of the borough's previous championships from 1859 to 1866 and again in 1868 and1869. All in all, it was a fitting nightcap to the town where baseball had first caught fire.

In 1900, Brooklyn was a far cry from the simpler times in 1801 when its children played their version of "stick and ball" in fields instead of on asphalt. But in other ways, the complexities added to the game had helped make it more elemental to the thousands who had come to enjoy and appreciate this most wonderful pastime.

20

THE CENTURY MAN

JUNE 20, 2008

In a normally quiet nursing home in Charlotte, North Carolina, approximately eighty people had gathered. Some were familiar friends whereas others were total strangers. At the center of their collective attention was a brand new centenarian.

His name...Billy Werber.

Billy's claims to fame were numerous. For one thing, he had become the final surviving teammate of Babe Ruth. Others primarily recognized him as the oldest living major leaguer.

Still others in the baseball world mostly saw him as one of the great base stealers from the 1930s—having led the American League in swipes on three occasions.

In attendance at the birthday party was Billy's seventy-seven-year-old son, who sweetly referred to his dad as having the sharp mind of an eighty year old. That's high praise for someone whose age has clicked all the way up to three digits.

Billy's uncommon lucidity was a special treat for his visitors...for if they were polite enough, they would be enriched with wonderful stories from his eleven seasons in the show.

They might have heard about how Billy handled contract negotiations in the spring of 1939.

Connie Mack, the tight-fisted owner and manager of the Philadelphia Athletics, had sent the third baseman a letter along with a renewal contract

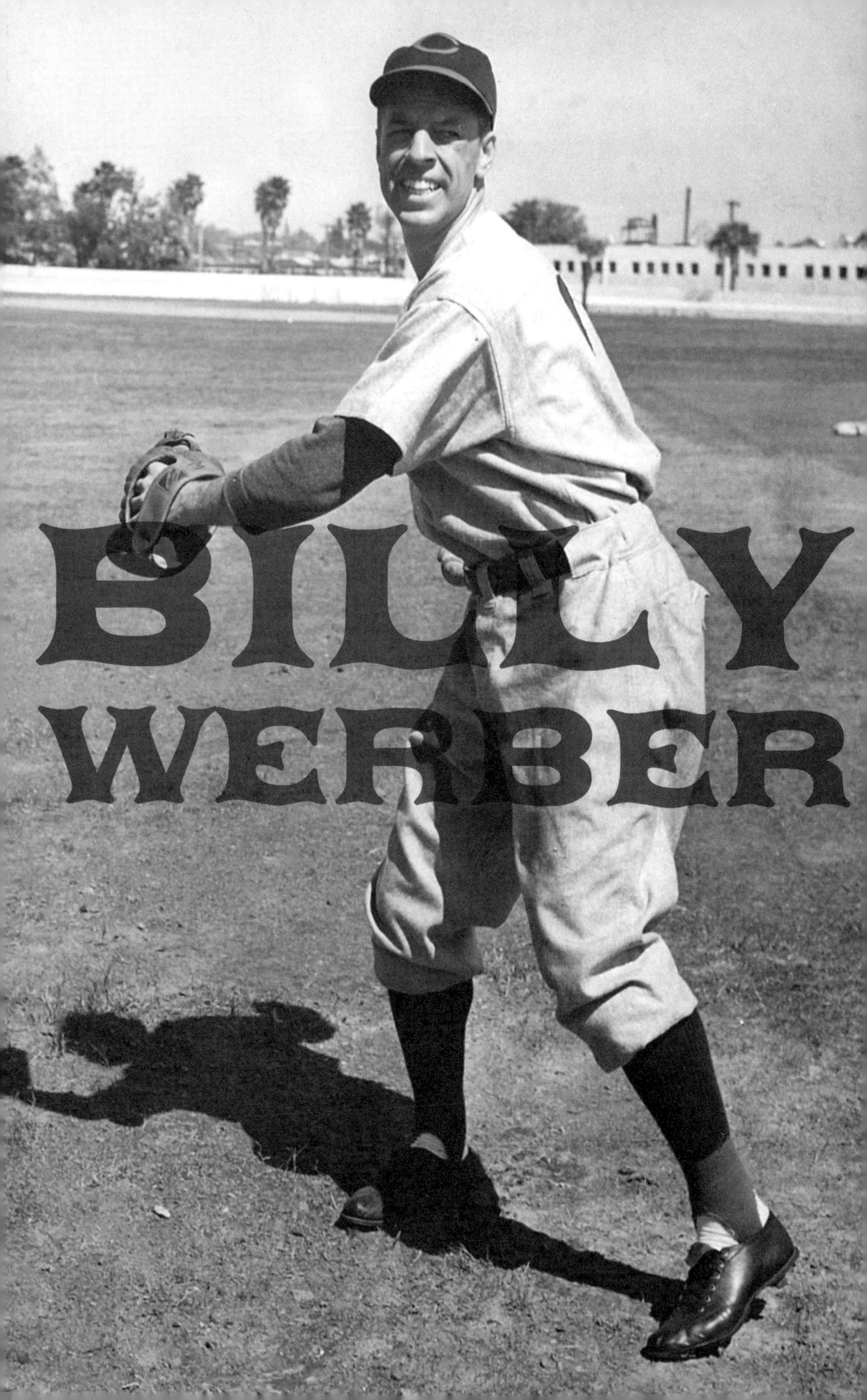
BILLY
WERBER

informing him that his pay had been cut. Mack's letter cited that the team had just come off a bad year, that they were anticipating another bad year, and that the team had been overpaid the year before.

In lieu of accepting Connie Mack's frugal offer, Werber had the gumption to write the following response to the powerful icon:

"In substance, Mr. Mack, what I would advise you to do is sell your ball club and get into a more profitable business."

Billy Werber never heard from Connie Mack. However, the Cincinnati Reds ball club did contact Billy to let him know that from that point forward, they would be in charge of signing his paychecks.

Billy ended up playing valuable roles for Cincy in the next two Fall Classics—and even picked up a ring the second time around. As for Connie Mack, both his 1939 and 1940 teams failed to post win percentages above .400.

Another wonderful source of amusement for Billy could be found whenever someone would ask him about the time he turned a walk into a triple. Here's how he pulled it off: A few steps prior to taking his base on balls, Billy broke into a bent sprint, scraped first, and beelined to second. The throw missed the mark and sailed into the outfield, allowing Billy to scamper to third. The element of surprise was rarely as strong as when he pulled off that particular shenanigan.

The subject of the New York Yankees could also light up Billy's centennial eyes. Second baseman Tony Lazzeri was one of his favorite teammates, in part because Tony was always good for a practical joke or two.

On one occasion, Tony had switched Babe Ruth's eyewash solution for water and then shocked the dumbfounded Ruth by casually drinking it down. Another time, Lazzeri introduced Ruth to one of their longtime teammates as though he was a brand new addition to the club freshly signed out of Harvard. The Babe, known for being completely oblivious to many of his lesser teammates, greeted the "newcomer" and heartily welcomed him aboard—despite the fact the man on the other end of the handshake had been a clubhouse fixture for four seasons.

Werber could recall the long train rides to Chicago and Detroit in which he would team up with Bill Dickey to play bridge against Babe Ruth and Lou Gehrig. Werber astutely remembered how the fun-loving Babe Ruth would inevitably torment the Iron Horse with what he called "funky bids." Ruth's wily methodology would often leave the highly irritated Gehrig with no choice but to fold his cards and settle off his debts to Werber and Dickey.

All told, Werber's life had been speckled with happy memories, both from baseball and from his other pastimes as well.

Though he was only 5´10″, Billy had been an All-American basketball player at Duke. In addition, he had authored three books, sold pension plans, and had even run a successful insurance business. A pillar of his family and community, Billy's many assists off the field no doubt surpassed the 2,695 assists he tallied on it.

On his hundredth birthday, he provided a tangible link to a bygone era. After all, he played four seasons at Fenway Park back when it was thought of as relatively modern. He was a New York Giant at the Polo Grounds. He even was elected a member of the Cincinnati Reds Hall of Fame long before the era of the Big Red Machine.

Besides all the aforementioned Hall of Famers, Billy Werber also rode the pine with Joe McCarthy, Bucky Harris, Joe Cronin, Bill McKechnie, Earl Combs, Red Ruffing, Joe Sewell, Mel Ott, Waite Hoyt, Herb Pennock, Heinie Manush, Lefty Gomez, Lefty Grove, Jimmie Foxx, Rick Ferrell, Ernie Lombardi, Lloyd Waner, Al Simmons, Carl Hubbell, and Johnny Mize. That's truly amazing company.

The great Billy Werber: once a young New York Yankee and forever a World Champion Cincinnati Red.

Billy was a valued teammate and a valid contributor. So in a sense, he is not so much from a bygone era, but from an adjacent time and place that will remain current in the minds of baseball fans for years to come.

On that day in June, it seemed like Billy would live forever. But on January 22, 2009, he passed away. Rest in peace, William "Billy" Murray Werber (1908-2009).

21

MICKEY MANTLE, WHITEY FORD, AND BILLY MARTIN GO HUNTING

◇◇◇

Much has been written about the legendary friendship between the Mick, Slick, and Billy. The trio played together for the Yankees from 1953 to 1957 and formed a bond that extended well beyond their playing years.

Culturally, they formed an unusual group. Mickey had grown up in rural Oklahoma whereas Whitey and Billy came of age on meaner streets (Queens and Berkeley respectively). But despite the diversity, they shared an appreciation for having fun and were no strangers to the idea of playing practical jokes on one another. Here's one of the stories Billy told.

At the end of the 1974 season, Billy had already distinguished himself as a manager. He had quickly turned around the fortunes of the Texas Rangers, and the entire region was very appreciative of the job he had done. His players knew of Billy's love for hunting and as a thank-you, they gave him a couple shotguns. Mantle, living near the Texas-Oklahoma border, heard the news and gave Billy a call. He mentioned to his old pal that he had a doctor friend in Texas with several hundred acres of land they could use for a hunting trip. It sounded like a plan.

When they got to the property, Mantle, Ford, and Martin drove up to the main house. Mantle excused himself to say hi to the doctor and to let him know of their presence. The doctor had no problem with the trio hunting on his land but seemed in an especially depressed mood. Mantle asked what was the matter.

The doctor said he had an old mule in a barn that had gone blind. It needed to be put down, but the doctor hadn't the heart to do it as the animal had become part of the family.

Mantle gently agreed to put the mule out of its misery so that his friend wouldn't have to do it. But on the way out of the house, the lightbulb above Mantle's head got especially bright. For this practical joke to work, he would have to really act up a storm.

Quickly feigning anger, he stomped back to his truck and threw himself inside. Whitey and Billy immediately wondered what had made Mickey so furious. Mickey told them that his friend had, for the first time ever, refused to grant him permission to hunt. Whitey and Billy wondered why.

Mickey slowly revealed that the doctor had peered outside, saw Whitey and Billy, and decided that he didn't want "their kind" on his land.

At this point, Billy's blood started to boil and Whitey wasn't all that happy either. As though he was defending their honor, Mickey then talked about his plan to fix his old friend but good.

Mickey whipped out of the car, followed by Billy and Whitey, and trudged into the barn, raised his gun up at the mule, and fired. The beast slumped lifelessly to the ground.

Despite the sad occasion, Mickey had to force himself not to laugh. He could hardly wait to turn around to see the expressions on his friends' faces and to then let them in on the joke.

But before he could spring the joke, he heard two shotgun blasts in rapid succession.

Worried about his friends, he wheeled around to see Billy with a wide grin on his face with smoke leaking from his shotgun.

"I got two of the bastard's cows!!"

22

THE KENNY LOFTON CURSE

Nowadays, the average major league ballplayer (who stays on the active roster the entire season) stands a 26.7 percent chance of making the playoffs.

For a player who strings together a thirteen-year career, it stands to reason that, on average, he will make it to the postseason 3.47 times. Of course, there are exceptions.

Damion Easley, most recently of the New York Mets, hasn't made it to the postseason in seventeen years in the bigs—despite playing with seven ball clubs with recent playoff histories (the Angels, Tigers, Rays, Marlins, Diamondbacks, and Mets).

On the flip side, the Yankees have made the playoffs in thirteen of Derek Jeter's first fourteen seasons. However, that high level of efficiency was sort of expected since the Yankees have carried the highest team payroll ever since Derek was a rookie.

But then, we have the strange case of outfielder Kenny Lofton.

From 1995 through 2007, Kenny reached the postseason eleven times, despite changing teams on eleven occasions during that span.

By the time he wrapped up his seventeen-year career, Kenny had played on nine division winners, two wild-card playoff teams, and been part of four other second-place ball clubs.

On one hand, Kenny Lofton could be seen as a catalyst who magically sparked his teams into playoff contention, but others could say that it was simply a case of top playoff contenders repeatedly seeing Kenny as the final piece to their puzzle.

But there is one thing that can't be disputed. Kenny won. He was part of Bobby Cox's fifteen-year glory period in Atlanta. He was part of Joe Torre's storied thirteen-year run in the Bronx. Here's another feather for his cap: the Cleveland Indians have had seven playoff teams since 1954 and Kenny was on six of them.

But despite his brains, talents, skills (and possibly his intangibles), somehow he never once played for a world champion. We will now investigate the evidence that has led some people to wonder about a "Kenny Lofton Curse."

1995 Cleveland Indians

In the deciding game of the World Series, Kenny Lofton's team is one-hit by Tom Glavine and loses the game by a score of 1-0. Though the Atlanta Braves of the 1990s played in five Fall Classics, this year proves to be the only one they would win, and Kenny is on the losing end of it.

1996 Cleveland Indians

In the divisional series against the Baltimore Orioles, the Tribe loses the deciding game in extra innings despite going into the ninth inning holding the lead.

1997 Atlanta Braves

If you can't beat them, join them, right? Wrong. The apparent curse jumps leagues as Kenny's team loses to the upstart Florida Marlins in the NLCS despite holding a 2-1 game advantage.

1998 Cleveland Indians

Kenny returns to his original Native-American franchise where they promptly roll over the Red Sox in the divisional series. However, the Indians blow a 2-1 ALCS advantage over the Yankees by losing three straight. For Kenny, it is a carbon copy of what happened the year before. Some begin to wonder if his career was somehow built on an ancient Indian burial site.

1999 Cleveland Indians

In the divisional series against the Boston Red Sox, the Tribe goes up two games to none but then lose three straight at Fenway Park to ensure their elimination. Boston averages in excess of 14 runs per game during the slaughter.

2001 Cleveland Indians
In the divisional series against the Seattle Mariners, the Tribe goes up 2-1, but then drops the final two games. Sensing a pattern here?

2002 San Francisco Giants
In what is possibly the highlight of his career, Kenny hits a lethal RBI single in the bottom of the ninth inning against the St. Louis Cardinals to put the Giants into the World Series. Against the Anaheim Angels, the winning momentum continues as Kenny's Giants go up 3-2 and even take a 5-run lead into the seventh inning of Game Six. With just 8 outs to go to reach the pinnacle, the Giants cannot stop the Angels, who come back to win. The Angels take Game Seven as well when closer Troy Percival induces Kenny to fly out to centerfield to end the game.

2003 Chicago Cubs
For the second consecutive season, Kenny Lofton plays for manager Dusty Baker and once again the tandem reaches the playoffs. They get by the Atlanta Braves in the first round and manage to take a 3-1 game lead in the NLCS against the wild-card Florida Marlins. However, Josh Beckett hurls a 2-hit shutout at them to take Game 5. In Game Six, the Cubbies take a 3-0 lead into the eighth inning.

With just 5 outs separating the Cubs from the Fall Classic, a ball sails into the stands that some people felt outfielder Moises Alou could have gotten to if not for fan interference. In subsequent plays, the Cubs melt down, and the Fish knock in 8 to take the lead and ultimately the game. This outcome sets the stage for a Game Seven. Lofton's Cubs take a 5-3 lead into the fifth inning, but end up losing the game to end their season and to dash the hopes of Cubs fans everywhere.

2004 New York Yankees

The Yankees and Red Sox match up for an historic ALCS. Par for the course, the Yankees continue their dominance by going up three games to nothing. However, the red sock of Curt Schilling inspires the other Red Sox to stick together, and the underdogs pull off a remarkable comeback. Once again, when all is said and done, Kenny Lofton is on the wrong side of the victory column.

2006 Los Angeles Dodgers

Kenny's team is quickly swept by the New York Mets. One wonders if Lofton wasn't relieved they didn't blow a lead.

2007 Cleveland Indians

Kenny returns to his primary team, where he helps them dispatch the Yankees in the divisional series. Against the Red Sox in the ALCS, the Tribe goes up by a margin of 3–1, but par for the course, they drop the final three games and are eliminated. Somewhat apropos, this series proves to be Kenny Lofton's swan song.

Follies Factoids

Kenny Lofton stole 622 bases over the course of his career. Outside of Cleveland, the locale where he most prolifically swiped bases was at US Cellular Field, the stadium nearest to the city where he grew up (East Chicago, Indiana).

Kenny Lofton is the all-time steals leader for both the Cleveland Indians AND for the University of Arizona Wildcats basketball team.

Tim Stoddard and Kenny Lofton are the only two men in history to play in college basketball's Final Four AND in the World Series.

23

LOU PINIELLA'S LESSON

◇◇

When Lou Piniella talks about winning, people listen. Five pennants and three rings have a way of lending gravity to a speaker. At one point during the 2008 season, the Chicago Cubs' manager thought back to his playing days.

"I remember one time, one manager told me I looked tired, and I agreed with him, and seventeen days later, I got back in the lineup. The guy who was playing for me did a heck of a job."

The lesson to be learned here by young players seems apparent enough. If your manager offers you a day off, refuse his kindness.

The article went on to surmise that the manager in question was Dick Howser and that the player who made it so hard for Lou to get back in was Oscar Gamble. We took it upon ourselves to look up even more history behind the anecdote.

It quickly became apparent that sweet Lou was indeed referring to Dick Howser and that the team was the 1980 Yankees. Lou was the primary Yankee left fielder and he hit .287 overall while managing to strike out a mere 20 times. But we dug through the records and found the facts to be slightly different.

There was a seventeen-game stretch in which Piniella only started once, but at no point was he left off the lineup cards for seventeen consecutive games. As to the identity of the ballplayer who spelled Piniella, we found that it couldn't have been Oscar Gamble because during this seventeen-game span, Oscar only appeared twice—and did so solely as a pinch-hitter.

It turns out the slack was mostly picked up by a platoon consisting of Yankee legend Bobby Murcer (who went 6 for 24) and young Joe Lefebvre (who hit .269 by going 7 for 26). That's solid play by both, but nothing extraordinary.

But even though fiction can sometimes be more dramatic than actual history, the lesson behind Lou's sweet anecdote remains as true as steel. Be a gamer.

A FOLLIES TRIVIA QUIZ ANSWERS *(from page 63)*

Answer 1: The thing that George Washington, Babe Ruth, Sparky Anderson, Tom Seaver, and Ken Griffey Jr. all have in common is that they all originally had the first name of George.

Answer 2: The four pitchers who managed to save one hundred games during both the 1970s and the 1980s are Gene Garber, Goose Gossage, Bruce Sutter, and myself, Rollie Fingers.

Answer 3: The first hitter to come up to the plate in the first baseball game ever televised was Billy Werber (the subject of chapter 18).

24

THE
RICKEY HENDERSON
DOSSIER

HENDERSON, Rickey

DOSSIER - 24

EARLY CHILDHOOD: Chicago/Oakland

BOYHOOD FACT: Born in the backseat of a 1957 Chevy

HIGH SCHOOL ACCOMPLISHMENTS: Played basketball and was also a heavily recruited All-American running back.

DRAFTED: Was the 96th pick in the 1976 June draft

ODD TRIVIA: One of the rare right-handed hitters who threw left-handed

PROS DRAFTED AHEAD OF HIM INCLUDED: Alan Trammell, Mike Scioscia, Mike Scott, Floyd Bannister, Bruce Hurst

MINOR LEAGUE GAMES BEFORE DEBUT: 384

MOST FREQUENT MINOR LEAGUE HOME: Modesto, California

MINOR LEAGUE TRIVIA: Once stole seven bases in one game

DEBUT YEAR: 1979

AGE AT DEBUT: 20

HENDERSON, Rickey

EARLIEST TEAMMATES INCLUDED: Tony Armas, Mitchell Page, Dave Revering

FINAL MLB SEASON: 2003

FINAL TEAMMATES INCLUDED: Kevin Brown, Eric Gagne, Shawn Green

PRIMARY MANAGER: Tony La Russa

TOTAL MANAGERS PLAYED FOR: 15

TOTAL SEASONS IN THE MAJOR LEAGUES: 25

NUMBER OF LOSING SEASONS: 9.5 (switched teams in midseason on four occasions)

CAREER STATS: .279 BA/297 HR/1,115 RBI

RUNS: 2,295 (first all-time)

WALKS: 2,190 (second all-time)

STOLEN BASES: 1,406 (first all-time)

GOLD GLOVE AWARDS: 1

HENDERSON, Rickey

REGULAR SEASON WINNING PERCENTAGE IN GAMES IN
WHICH RICKEY PARTICIPATED: 51%

POSITIONS PLAYED (rounded):

LF	77%	PH	4%
CF	14%	RF	1%
DH	5%		

MAJOR LEAGUE AFFILIATIONS (rounded):

Oakland A's (55%)	Boston Red Sox (2%)
New York Yankees (19%)	Toronto Blue Jays (1%)
San Diego Padres (17%)	Anaheim Angels (1%)
New York Mets (5%)	Los Angeles Dodgers (1%)
Seattle Mariners (3%)	

INJURY OR REST RATE: 20%

BEST SEASON:
(1985) .314 BA/24 HR/72 RBI/146 RUNS/80 SB

PLAYOFF RECORD:
8 postseasons—60 games
222 AT-BATS: .284 BA/5 HR/20 RBI/47 RUNS/33 SB
3 pennants
2 world championships

ALL-STAR TEAMS: 10

HENDERSON, Rickey

DOSSIER - 24

ALL-STAR STATS:
24 AT-BATS: .292 BA/0 HR/1 RBI/3 RUNS/2 SB

TRADED: 4 times

SIGNED WITH A TEAM AS A FREE AGENT: 9 times

MOST FREQUENT FOE:
Frank Tanana - 117 plate appearances
(.350 BA/11 HR/18 RBI)

THE PITCHER HE HOMERED MOST OFTEN AGAINST:
Frank Tanana (11)

THE PITCHER HE WALKED MOST OFTEN AGAINST:
Randy Johnson (26)

THE PITCHER HE OWNED:
Jimmy Key: .409 (36 for 88) with 9 HRs, 14 RBIs, 13
walks and 8 strikeouts

THE PITCHER WHO OWNED HIM:
Roger Clemens: .167 (11 for 66) with 0 HRs, 2 RBIs, 13
walks and 19 strikeouts

THE PITCHER HE STRUCK OUT MOST OFTEN AGAINST:
Randy Johnson (30)

HENDERSON, Rickey

DOSSIER - 24

LEAGUE STOLEN BASE CHAMPION: 12 times

LEAGUE MVP: 1 time

MOST FREQUENT OPPONENT: California/Anaheim Angels

HOME AWAY FROM HOME:
Cleveland
.337 BA/14 HR/44 RBI/91 RUNS/71 WALKS/61 SB

CLOSEST STATISTICAL TWIN: Craig Biggio

HALL OF FAME CALIBRE RATING: 144%

Follies Factoids

Rickey Henderson, the all-time stolen base champion, has 49.9% more steals than Lou Brock, the player who is second on the list.

Rickey Henderson happened to be Nolan Ryan's 5,000th strikeout victim.

On the day that Rickey Henderson broke the all-time record for stolen bases, Nolan Ryan overshadowed the occasion by pitching one of his no-hitters.

In 1978-1979, Rickey Henderson played winter ball for a team in the Mexican Pacific League. With Rickey aboard, they won their first championship in thirty years.

The day Rickey Henderson collected his 3,000th hit coincided with teammate Tony Gwynn's final game as a player.

It's very likely that Rickey Henderson would have ended up with two league MVP awards (instead of one) if a certain relief pitcher (who shall humbly go unmentioned here) hadn't won the overall voting in 1981.

25

THE BENCHMARK

<><><><><><><><><><><><><><><><><><><><><><><><><><><><><><><><><><><><><>

JUNE 20, 2008

On this date, the World Series came to Oakland for the first time. The Cincinnati Reds were in town for Game Three. At that moment in time, neither group of players had won a single World Championship ring, but over the course of the next five years, we would combine to win them all.

Our skipper was Dick Williams. Five years earlier he had guided the Boston Red Sox to the pennant, so this was familiar territory for him. The Reds had their own future Hall of Fame manager in Sparky Anderson. Like Williams, Sparky had also managed to bring his team all the way to the Fall Classic without winning it.

Over forty-nine thousand people were packed into the Oakland Coliseum. There was some added drama because we were suddenly without the extraordinary talents of Reggie Jackson. Unfortunately for us, Reggie had torn his hamstring stealing home in the divisional series.

It turned into a very tight game. Blue Moon Odom held the Reds to 3 hits and 1 run over seven innings despite the presence of such great Reds players as Pete Rose, Joe Morgan, and Tony Perez.

In contrast, Cincinnati starter Jack Billingham kept us from scoring a single run, so the Reds were beating us 1–0.

The top of the eighth inning started with Vida Blue in relief.

Blue relieved Blue Moon, to pitch to Rose, who lined out to Dick Green, our second baseman. But little did we know that the game was about to get a lot more colorful.

Joe Morgan came up and worked Vida for a walk. Then Bobby Tolan smacked a solid single that sent Morgan to third.

Dick Williams then made the call to bring me into the game. It was a different era for closers, as we often came in even when it was only the seventh or eighth inning—even when it wasn't a save situation.

The first batter I faced was Johnny Bench, a hitter I had never faced before. Here was a guy coming off a monster season who was about to be named the National League's Most Valuable Player.

My count to Bench quickly went to 2 balls and 2 strikes. It was looking to many like the Reds were about to break the game wide open, especially when Tolan stole second on my next offering to Bench, which wound up in the dirt.

You just have to know that Dick Williams' mind was whirling away at a thousand miles an hour. Somehow, he was reminded of an ancient trick play used by a Cardinals' manager from the 1940s named Billy Southworth. With first base suddenly open, anyone with an ounce of common sense would walk the powerful Bench. Most everyone in the Coliseum (and watching at home) was expecting that very move.

Williams sprung into action by darting out to the mound. He launched into an animated performance that convinced everyone he was chewing me out for having given a hitter as dangerous as Bench anything to hit at all. Simultaneously, he began miming that he was calling for the intentional walk—what he was really doing was telling Gene Tenace and myself how to catch the Reds' catcher offguard.

Gene Tenace and I had been given our orders. Gene was to stand away from the plate and motion for the intentional pass. Then, I was to throw the ball right down the middle. Gene would somehow have to get back behind the plate in time to make sure my pitch wouldn't sail to the backstop, which would allow Joe Morgan to speed home. Also, Gene had to make sure he didn't move behind the plate too early lest he tip off Bench to what we were up to.

On his way off the mound, Dick then whispered some advice I didn't need.

"Be sure you throw a breaking ball, because if it's a fastball and some-body figures out what we're doing, Bench can hit the sh#@ out of it."

Gene and I didn't know what to think of Williams' decision, but we did know that we were going to try it out just the same. He trotted back behind the plate, walked a few steps to the side and motioned for a casual toss. Of course, it would be far from casual…it would be my slider. However, right before my windup, both Joe Morgan and the Reds' third base coach, Alex Grammas, smelled something amiss. They began to yell urgently for Johnny Bench to stay ready.

Uh oh.

Tenace broke at exactly the right time. He slid behind the plate and caught my slider on the outside corner. Bench, with his bat casually resting on his shoulder, watched in shocked horror as the umpire made the call.

Strike Three.

The Oakland Coliseum ……… came …………….. unglued!!!

In retrospect, I'd say that it was actually the best slider I had ever thrown in my entire life. Even I was surprised at the movement I got on that pitch—maybe even more surprised than Bench was when I threw it.

What ended up happening?

Well, I managed to keep the Reds from scoring that inning, but they took the victory all the same, so I guess you could say that our trickery didn't really pay us any dividends.

As for Johnny Bench and I, we laugh about it to this day. Here's a quote from John that always makes me smile:

"Fingers called it his best slider, did he? Great. But why does he have to do it to me? There's sixty million people out there watching."

As an incredible footnote of sorts, thirty-five years after my infa-mous phantom slider, Dick Williams got a phone call. It was from the Veteran's Committee. He had finally been voted into the Hall of Fame. The man who was elected to Cooperstown alongside him was the long-deceased Billy Southworth, who had inspired our ruse. How's that for irony?

Follies Factoids

1972 wouldn't be the last time that Dick Williams squared off against Sparky Anderson in the World Series. They met again in 1984 when Dick's San Diego Padres took on Sparky's Detroit Tigers.

While managing the California Angels, Dick Williams once moved batting practice into the lobby of the hotel where the team was staying and replaced the baseballs with whiffle balls. When his hitters questioned the move, he explained that the way they had been hitting, there was no risk of them breaking anything in the lobby. The team's hitting improved almost immediately.

Here are the teams that Dick Williams either played for or managed over the course of his thirty-four seasons in the major leagues:

Montreal Expos: 727 games
San Diego Padres: 649 games
Boston Red Sox: 617 games
Oakland Athletics: 478 games
Baltimore Orioles: 447 games

Seattle Mariners: 351 games
California Angels: 341 games
Kansas City Athletics: 257 games
Brooklyn Dodgers: 112 games
Cleveland Indians: 67 games

26

WE DON'T NEED NO STINKIN' PITCH COUNTS

◇◇

1979

The Oakland A's lost 108 games and finished in last place in the AL West.
Their young starting rotation of
MIKE NORRIS,
MATT KEOUGH,
RICK LANGFORD,
STEVE McCATTY,
AND BRIAN KINGMAN
(NKLMK)
combined for only 38 wins, 840 innings, and a 4.52 ERA.

1980

Billy Martin took over the reigns of the Oakland A's.
Although the roster was largely unchanged from the season before,
the A's became winners and finished in second place in the AL West.
The team batting average rose 20 points
and the starting rotation of **NKLMK**
combined for 79 wins,
1,257 innings (an average of 251.1 innings per starter)
and a 3.23 ERA.
BRIAN KINGMAN
was the only one of Billy's five starters who didn't end up pitching a
fourteen-inning complete game.

All told, **NKLMK**
pitched 85.5% of their team's innings,
completed 93 out of 162 games (57%),
and averaged 7.2 innings per start.

1981

During this strike-interrupted year, Oakland's rotation improved even
more and advanced to the ALCS (before being swept by the Yankees).
As for **NKLMK**,
they pitched 80.0% of their team's innings,
completed 59 out of 109 games,
posted a 3.20 ERA,
and averaged 7.1 innings per start.

OKAY, MAYBE WE DO NEED STINKIN' PITCH COUNTS

1982

The A's slid into fifth place.
Neither **STEVE McCATTY** nor **BRIAN KINGMAN**
could pitch as many as 130 innings and
Mike Norris fell short of 170.
All told, **NKLMK**
combined for only 39 wins, 864.1 innings
and posted a 4.69 ERA.
They pitched 59.4% of their team's innings and
completed 37 out of 162 games (23%).

AFTERMATH

Due to the excessive wear and tear, all five pitchers suffered
physically. The 1982 season became the final time that
RICK LANGFORD (thirty years old),
MIKE NORRIS (twenty-seven years old)
BRIAN KINGMAN (twenty-seven years old)
and **MATT KEOUGH** (twenty-six years old)
were able to throw as many as 100 innings.
As for **STEVE McCATTY**,
he pitched three more years before
retiring at the age of thirty-one, but 1982 proved to be
the last season in which he posted a winning record.

27

WHAT STAYS IN VEGAS, HAPPENS IN MILWAUKEE

March 31, 1970

The Seattle Pilots walked off the field in Tempe, Arizona, after losing to the California Angels 4-2.

An unusual discomfort accompanied this loss, not because games count for much in spring training, but because none of the Pilot players were certain of their futures. Normally, a couple guys are still on the bubble when camp breaks, but in this case, the entire team was on it.

The team's anchors included manager Dave Bristol, who had moved over from the Reds organization, and Tommy Harper, the club's speedy third baseman. But even they didn't know whether they were destined for Seattle or Milwaukee.

Another rumor swirling around claimed that the entire team might go bankrupt, which would essentially make everyone a free agent. All in all, it was a bad time for anyone who had signed an apartment lease in Seattle.

Shortly after the last Pilot left the clubhouse, the attendants finished gathering up everything that wasn't nailed down. Soon, it was all loaded into trucks for the long haul to parts unknown.

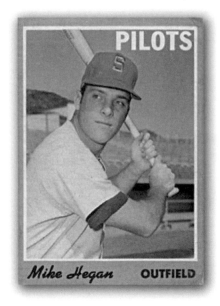
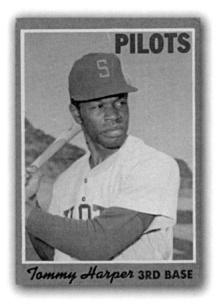

When these 1970 Topps cards hit the stores, the Pilots already had flown away.

APRIL 1, 1970

Early on, the moving trucks hit Las Vegas. At the time, the city wasn't even one-tenth the size of the megopolis it is today, but in its adolescence, it still had its fair share of feather-clad showgirls, one-armed bandits, and all-you-can-eat buffets.

If Sin City wasn't disorienting enough, the truck driver's orders were. He was told that everyone should stay in Vegas and wait for word about which direction to travel. Would they head northwest so the equipment could be used for the sophomore season of the Seattle Pilots? Or, would they drive northeast for the inaugural season of the Milwaukee Brewers? At the time, no one knew for sure.

Hedging their bets, the trucks were told to continue north on a slightly eastern route before finally staging in Provo, Utah.

There was no practical point in going any farther from this fork in the road until they knew their destiny.

Though this hadn't been intended as an April Fool's Day prank, it played out like one. With the opening of the regular season just a few days away, truckloads of major league equipment sat idle and direction-less in Provo, Utah.

FLASHBACK TO 1969

The first (and last) Seattle Pilots season had been a bit of a disaster. They played their games in Sick's Stadium, a minor league facility so behind in upgrades that some Opening Day fans had to wait three innings for their benches to be installed.

In addition, the water pressure was so low on the joint's plumbing that the toilets would go on strike whenever too many men would have to see about too many horses. On these occasions, the stadium's name was never as apropos.

It probably didn't help matters that the Pilots had the highest ticket and concession food prices in the sport, and they lacked a local television contract.

Did I mention that they were a last-place team? Did I mention that the minority owner warned fans that they would move the team if the attendance didn't pick up?

Tensions had been sky high between the Seattle owner and the local political leaders. At various points:

- The owner refused to pay the city rent.
- The city threatened to evict the club.
- Creditors hounded the Seattle owner.
- Lawsuits were delaying the completion of a major league domed facility and a petition doomed an alternative locale.
- A new ownership group that wanted to keep the team in Seattle fell apart almost as fast as they came together.

EARLY 1970

A wealthy thirty-five-year-old car dealer from Milwaukee made the scenario even more interesting. He was a baseball fanatic by the name of Bud Selig, and he had been making a furtive play to relocate the Pilots since October of the previous year.

But Bud had company. Another prospective owner out of Dallas had also thrown his hat into the ring to hijack the Pilots as well. However, they both appeared foiled when the State of Washington entered the picture to unveil an injunction prohibiting the team from leaving the state.

But there were more flies yet to hit the ointment.

In March, as the Pilot players worked out in the Arizona sun, the team filed for bankruptcy. Some would say they were leaking money like a sieve, but others felt that it was merely a shrewd maneuver designed to break the state's injunction.

The League was especially worried. They didn't want one of their teams forfeiting all of its games, nor did they want all the Pilot players and many of their employees on the free-agent block.

On April 1, the Federal Bankruptcy referee approved the bankruptcy—which cleared the way for Bud Selig to purchase the team—which cleared the way for the moving trucks to leave Provo for Milwaukee.

April 7, 1970

The baseball rolled off the hand of Lew Krausse, and with it began the rebirth of baseball in Milwaukee. There were 36,107 fans on hand for Opening Day at County Stadium. Few minded that the team was playing in hastily modified uniforms with the imprints of the old Pilot logos still visible.

It was a healing experience as the Milwaukee fans had been without major league baseball for four long seasons—ever since their beloved Braves had departed for Atlanta.

It was their brave deliverance.

Follies Factoids

After the Pilots flew the coop, Seattle went without major league baseball for seven seasons. The drought ended in 1977 with the debut of the Seattle Mariners, who had a fully functional domed stadium waiting for them.

The Pilots were one of only two teams in the modern era to have spent a single year in the major leagues before moving on to a new city. The other? The Milwaukee Brewers, who played the 1901 season in the new American League before moving south to become the St. Louis Browns.

Besides the three major league incarnations of the Milwaukee Brewers, there was also a notable minor league version that played from 1902 to 1952. In its final years, the team was the Class AAA affiliate for the Boston Braves.

Bud Selig's ownership group reportedly paid between ten and thirteen million dollars for the Seattle Pilots. That was roughly the same amount of money it cost to produce the top film of 1970 (*Airport*) and near the cost of many Las Vegas casinos of the era.

28

LITTLE KNOWN FACTS ABOUT BUD SELIG

◇◇

March 31, 1970

Bud Selig is perhaps most famous for his role as baseball's commissioner—a job he undertook in 1992. Although he has been a lightning rod for controversy from time to time, he will probably go down in history for contributing to the sport's rise into a realm of unprecedented popularity, profit, and expansion.

Allan "Bud" Selig was born in 1934 in Milwaukee, the city in which he still lives.

From 1939 to 1945, the local minor league team (the Milwaukee Brewers) funneled its best players to the Chicago Cubs. During these formative years, young Bud first became a rabid fan. This Brewer team would go on to be a farm club for the Boston Braves. To the delight of the teenaged Bud, Milwaukee thrilled its fans by winning the Junior World Series in both 1947 and 1951.

For numerous reasons, 1952 was a big year for Bud. He turned eighteen, went off to college in nearby Madison to study history and political science, and the Boston Braves moved to town bringing major league baseball with them.

By the time the decade ended, Bud had graduated from college,

had served two years in the armed forces, had cut his teeth working for his father's lucrative car leasing company, and had even worked his way into becoming a minority shareholder in the Milwaukee Braves franchise.

Key players for this ball club included Henry Aaron, Eddie Mathews, Warren Spahn, Lew Burdette, and Red Schoendienst.

The highlight year for the team occurred in 1957 when the Braves took out the New York Yankees in seven games. Both beer *and* champagne flowed throughout Wisconsin when that happened.

But after fourteen seasons of thrilling their fans, the Braves majority owner decided to move on to Atlanta. Despite Bud Selig's best efforts, he was powerless to stop the move.

Crushed, he sold all of his stock in the Braves and immediately began an ambitious campaign to bring major league baseball back to Milwaukee. Almost like an event promoter, Selig engineered for some preseason games to be played in Milwaukee, many of which drew in excess of fifty-one thousand fans.

In 1968 and 1969, Selig had even maneuvered the Chicago White Sox into playing some of their regular season games in Milwaukee—where the team drew larger crowds than they did back home. His plan was to relocate the White Sox north to Milwaukee, and he made major inroads toward this quest, but Major League Baseball struck him down in their own best interests.

It was at this point, that Selig successfully targeted the Seattle Pilots; the team had prematurely come into existence so that the expansion Kansas City Royals could have a symmetrical bookend. As you know from reading the previous chapter, Selig got his way.

Seven times under Selig's ownership watch, the Brewers were awarded "Organization of the Year," and his reputation as a highly efficient team owner began to spread around baseball.

The peak of the Milwaukee Brewers during the Bud Selig years was in 1982. Loaded with talent and grit, my Brewer teammates not only won the AL pennant, they actually came within 11 outs of winning it all. Cecil Cooper, Jim Gantner, Paul Molitor, Ben Oglivie, Ted Simmons, Don Sutton, Gorman Thomas, Pete Vuckovich, Ned Yost, and Robin Yount were just some of the key players that season who, to this day, never have to pay for their own beers within Milwaukee city limits. (Well, okay...maybe Gantner does).

As time rolled on, Selig slowly phased himself out as a team owner in order to become the economic czar of baseball. On his watch, we've seen the introduction of three division leagues, wild-card playoff spots, inter-league play, and the introduction of eighteen new modernized ball yards.

Sure, he's had his detractors, but all in all Selig is a fan favorite in Milwaukee, which probably wouldn't even have baseball if not for the efforts of one of its most rabid fans.

Follies Factoids

In 1950, Milwaukee was the thirteenth-largest city in the United States. But even so, it was largely bereft of pro sports save for minor league baseball and for the three times per year that the Packers came to town. But in 1951, the NBA arrived in the form of the Milwaukee Hawks. In 1952, professional IHL hockey arrived in the form of the Milwaukee Chiefs. Then, in 1953, the Boston Braves moved west to become the Milwaukee Braves. It sure was a good time to be a Milwaukee sports fan.

Well, sort of. In four years the Hawks finished last four times, compiling a record of 91 – 190 before moving to St. Louis. The Chiefs finished last both times in their two-year stay, with a record of 28 – 90 – 6. Maybe they weren't such *Happy Days* in Milwaukee in the 1950s.

29

CLOSE BUT NO AWARD

◇◇

IT'S RELATIVELY EASY TO FIND OUT WHICH PLAYER HAS AMASSED THE
MOST MVP AWARDS (BARRY BONDS WITH SEVEN).
IT'S A SIMILAR PIECE OF CAKE TO FIND OUT WHO HAS RACKED
UP THE HIGHEST TOTAL NUMBER OF CY YOUNG AWARDS
(ROGER CLEMENS WITH SEVEN).

BUT HAVE YOU EVER WONDERED WHO HAS FINISHED
IN SECOND PLACE FOR THESE PRESTIGIOUS AWARDS MOST OFTEN?
WE HAVE, AND HERE ARE THE ANSWERS.

Total Number of Second-Place Finishes for the Various MVP Awards
(1911-1914, 1922-2008)

*(The list includes those with a minimum of two second-place finishes.
I've included the number of MVP Awards they did win in parentheses)*

FOUR TIME RUNNERS-UP

Stan Musial (3)   Ted Williams (2)

THREE TIME RUNNERS-UP

Mickey Mantle (3)   Albert Pujols (2)

TWO TIME RUNNERS-UP

Luke Appling (0) ✗   Yogi Berra (3)

Barry Bonds (7)   George Brett (1)

Eddie Collins (1)   Andre Dawson (1)

Dizzy Dean (1)   Joe DiMaggio (3)

Cecil Fielder (0) ‹   Lou Gehrig (2)

Al Kaline (0) ✗   Chuck Klein (1)

Sandy Koufax (1)   Greg Luzinski (0)

Eddie Mathews (0) ✗   Willie Mays (2)

Johnny Mize (0)   Eddie Murray (0)

Tony Oliva (0)   Mike Piazza (0)

Alex Rodriguez (3)   Joe Rudi (0)

Willie Stargell (1)   Billy Williams (0)

Total Number of Second-Place Finishes for the Cy Young Award
(1956-2008)

(Includes those with a minimum of two second-place finishes. I've included the number of Cy Young Awards they did win in parentheses)

THREE TIME RUNNERS-UP

Randy Johnson (5)   Curt Schilling (0)

Warren Spahn (1)

TWO TIME RUNNERS-UP

Tom Glavine (2)   Trevor Hoffman (0)

Ferguson Jenkins (1)   Tommy John (0)

Jimmy Key (0)   Pedro Martinez (3)

Jim Palmer (3)   Dan Quisenberry (0)

Tom Seaver (3)

30

MILTON BRADLEY: A LIFE IN RETROSPECT

<><><><><><><><><><><><><><><><><><><><><><><><><><><><><><><><><><>

W hen the name of baseball player Milton Bradley is mentioned, many different images spring to mind. Some think of his overall expertise as a switch hitter. Others think of his 2008 season, in which he played so well for the Texas Rangers that he was selected to start in the All-Star Game. Some recall his clutch performance from the 2006 ALCS in which he went 9 for 18 and slugged .944 against the tough Minnesota Twins.

Still others think of his occasionally confrontational attitude, which may have contributed to the fact that he ended up playing for six different ball clubs within his first nine seasons. Stories have even surfaced that, for some reason we can't fathom, Milton has been teased because of his name.

We thought we would investigate Milton Bradley's life history to look for clues as to what may have contributed toward both his overall excellence as a baseball player and his reputation for having a fiery temper.

As it turns out, Milton endured some incredible hardships as a young man. For one thing, his home had neither electricity nor any modern convenience of any kind. In a sense, it was as though his home was from another century.

milton bradley

CHICAGO CUBS
OUTFIELD

As a youngster, he found work as a draftsman for the railroads, and it was at this point that he first crossed paths with patent seekers who shared his interests both in developing innovations and in seeking wealth. It was apparent that Milton was already on the path toward becoming noteworthy.

In his spare time, he taught himself the crafts of printing and lithographing and one day, inspiration struck. He produced a tremendous lithograph of a clean-shaven Abraham Lincoln, and it looked to be a certainty that the visage would soon sell like hotcakes because Lincoln was gaining in popularity.

However, after the classy pictures were produced, Lincoln decided to grow a beard and Abe's grooming decision completely screwed up Milton's get-rich-quick plan.

It was a tough break, but all great baseballers roll with the punches and Milton was no exception. Quickly, he turned his attention to an alternate project that might offset his earlier financial boondoggle.

Mirroring his own misfortune, he produced *The Checkered Game of Life*—the precursor to the modern board game. This game was novel in part because it had a top-like numerical die that could be spun around like a roulette wheel. He ambitiously set out to market his invention on the bustling streets of New York City.

What happened?

He sold through all two hundred of them in less than two days. Knowing he was onto something, he made more and in the winter of '60–'61, more than forty thousand units sold at many of the Northeast's finest stores. It was that Christmas season's version of *Tickle Me Elmo*, but Milton's creation was no fad, for the game evolved into what we know now as *The Game of Life*, which still sells like gangbusters today.

Milton earned lots of bucks for his invention, which came in handy since he was still years away from becoming a million-dollar ballplayer for the likes of the A's, Dodgers, Rangers, and Cubs.

As for his pursuits outside of helping his team win games, he gives back to the community by running baseball academies in the region of Los Angeles where he grew up.

Nowadays, Milton Bradley no longer has anything to do with the brand that bears his name, as it was long ago sold to a larger company. In fact, he's more of a fan of dominos than he is of board games. So, all in all, it's probably for the best that you should cross paths with Milton, you not mention his previous occupations before he played major league ball.

31

BERNIE BREWER VERSUS THE MIGRATORY CUBS

◇◇◇

It may seem like fun and games, but being a major league mascot isn't exactly the easiest job in the world.

For starters, your vision is impaired. Secondly, you must carry around so much extra girth that every day feels like the morning after Thanksgiving dinner. Finally, your outfit operates like a Caribbean sauna. Three hours inside of a gamey headpiece that smells like Limburger cheese can't be anyone's idea of paradise!

But in Milwaukee, there are a couple other added degrees of difficulty, and the guy who must undertake them is known as Bernie Brewer. How can I describe him for you?

He is very friendly and waves a lot. He wears lederhosen.

He is a mute. Hmm…what else? Basically, Bernie is your average, ordinary, eight-fingered, size-sixteen-shoe-wearing freak with green eyes bigger than limes. He also has a canary yellow moustache so big that it needs its own zip code. You know the type.

Although Bernie has been known to stop in at a tailgate party or two, for the most part, he doesn't roam the stands or perch on the tops of dugouts and cheerlead like so many of his counterparts. Instead, he spends much of the game high above left field inside of his own personal dugout.

Then, whenever a Brewer player hits it out of the park, Bernie hits a button that triggers fireworks, does a bowling kick, and then propels himself down a slippery slide into his own version of home plate. People in Milwaukee love the routine, and it might be the only venue in the majors where most of the fans' eyes don't follow the home run trot of the player.

In earlier times, Bernie did something even more unique. Upon every Brewer home run, he would slide down into what appeared to be a huge mug of beer. Balloons would even be blown out of the contraption to give the appearance of beer suds. It was a big hit...and literally, the toast of the town.

But in these more politically correct times, Bernie may still brew, but he no longer drinks.

This is apparently an effort to discourage youngsters from drinking beer at Miller Park in Milwaukee. But even more importantly, the change in Bernie's routine may help curb impressionable children from ever wanting to slide themselves down into an oversized frosty beverage.

As you know by now, being a mascot isn't easy, but in Milwaukee there is an added degree of difficulty built into the equation.

Cubs fans.

Like bears drawn to honey, many from Chicagoland drive up to Milwaukee whenever the Cubs visit Miller Park. For some fans, it's even more convenient, since getting tickets to Wrigley Field is not nearly as affordable and easy as it used to be.

Although most of these migratory Cubs fans are locked in on the game, some of them instead target Bernie with their jeering and heckling. In a way, it seems unfair because Bernie can't really talk.

His only preliminary weapons are to kind of affably wave at them or to ignore their cruel taunts completely.

Of course, the civility line gets crossed on occasion, which has led many a Cubs fan to get ejected from the ballpark upon Bernie giving the signal. It just goes to prove the old saying: never moon a man in lederhosen.

As for Cubs fans, I would think they'd try to befriend Bernie as much as possible. After all, no team in baseball seems to have been under the spell of a curse as long as the Cubbies. If they provided Bernie with gift baskets filled with Mountain Dew and deodorant sticks they might be able to reverse their bad luck. After all, the last thing they need is a hex from a mascot to go along with the curse of the Billy Goat that they already endure.

Follies Factoids

Only the Angels, Cubs, Dodgers, and Yankees do not utilize mascots.

Although Anaheim, Los Angeles, Milwaukee, and Toronto are represented by Major League Baseball, they are not represented by the National Football League (though Toronto does host some Buffalo Bills games). In addition, Chicago has two baseball teams but only one football team.

The NFL areas that are not represented by MLB are Buffalo, Charlotte, Green Bay, Jacksonville, Indianapolis, Nashville, and New Orleans.

Dolphin Stadium in Miami, the Metrodome in Minneapolis, and the Oakland-Alameda County Coliseum are the only three remaining facilities that host both MLB and the NFL.

32

THE BIGGEST NORTH AMERICAN REGIONS WITHOUT MAJOR LEAGUE BASEBALL

◇◇

There are thirty Major League Baseball teams. These thirty almost always play their home games in twenty-six metropolitan areas. One might think that it stands to figure that each of the top twenty-six metropolitan areas would get to host Major League Baseball, but that is not the case.

Whether it is because of traditions, economics, lack of a proper facility, or regional inconveniences, it's evident that having a massive population base simply does not guarantee you a team.

Currently, the Milwaukee Brewers play in the smallest major league market of all (and the KC Royals aren't far behind). The Brew Crew has the added disadvantage of playing close to Chicago. In fact, the triangulation of Miller Park, Wrigley Field, and U.S. Cellular Park is the smallest in all of baseball.

How relatively "mid-sized" is the Milwaukee market? Well, the city that hosts their Class AAA team (Nashville) is nearly equal in population—and it will eventually surpass Brew City.

But even so, few would argue that Milwaukee doesn't deserve their team. After all, they have a great facility, play in a town that loves them, and in recent years have proven themselves to be very competitive. So there's something to be said for the old maxim, at least in baseball, that size doesn't matter.

But just for drill, we've made a list of the fourteen US cities (and thirteen non-US metro areas on the continent) that have even larger population bases than Milwaukee.

Hypothetically, if you had to award another round of expansion franchises, which of the two following regions would you grant them to?

THE TOP 25 NORTH AMERICAN POPULATION ZONES THAT DO NOT CURRENTLY HOST MAJOR LEAGUE BASEBALL

(not including Central American cities)

1. **Mexico City, Mexico**
2. **Guadalajara, Mexico**
3. **Inland Empire of Southern California (Riverside-San Bernardino-Ontario)** *(37 miles from the Angels)*
4. **Monterrey, Mexico**
5. **Montreal, Canada** *(251 miles from the Red Sox)*
6. **San Juan, Puerto Rico**
7. **Santo Domingo, Dominican Republic**
8. **Havana, Cuba**
9. **Portland, Oregon** *(175 miles from the Mariners)*
10. **Juarez, Mexico / El Paso, Texas** *(436 miles from the Diamondbacks)*
11. **Vancouver, Canada** *(141 miles from the Mariners)*
12. **Puebla-Tlaxcala, Mexico**
13. **Sacramento, California** *(82 miles from the A's)*
14. **Orlando, Florida** *(106 miles from the Rays)*
15. **San Antonio, Texas** *(199 miles from the Astros)*
16. **Las Vegas, Nevada** *(265 miles from the Angels)*
17. **Northern California (South Bay: San Jose-Santa Clara-Sunnyvale)** *(36 miles from the A's)*
18. **Columbus, Ohio** *(110 miles from the Reds)*
19. **Port Au Prince, Haiti**
20. **Indianapolis, Indiana** *(113 miles from the Reds)*

21. **Hampton Roads, Virginia (Virginia Beach-Norfolk-Newport News)** *(177 miles from the Nats)*
22. **Charlotte, North Carolina** *(246 miles from the Braves)*
23. **Toluca, Mexico**
24. **Providence, Rhode Island** *(50 miles from the Red Sox)*
25. **Austin, Texas** *(160 miles from the Astros)*

Follies Factoids

The Cubs and White Sox play their home games 9.9 miles apart. The Mets and Yankees play their home games 10.1 miles apart. The A's and Giants play their home games 17.6 miles apart (by car). The Angels and Dodgers play their home games 31.1 miles apart.

The second-smallest triangulation of Major League Baseball stadiums (after Chicago-Chicago-Milwaukee) is New York-New York-Philadelphia.

Follies Preview: Can you name the relief pitcher who posted the most saves during the 1950s? (Can you also name the saves leader for each subsequent decade as well?) The answers are in the pages ahead.

Follies Puzzle: If you were at Turner Field in Atlanta and you had to go to the nearest major league stadium (other than Turner Field) what city would you depart for? (A clue appears on page 134)

33

THE NIEKRO BROTHERS

◇◇

In 1979, only two men in the National League were able to post as many as twenty-one victories—and they were both named Niekro.

Phil and Joe Niekro had a few other similarities as well.

They had both been schooled by their father on the art of the knuckler. They both played major league ball from 1967 to 1987. They were both all-stars. Both had stops with the Atlanta Braves (Phil's lasted nineteen seasons whereas Joe's stint was two years), and both were also teammates on the New York Yankees in 1985.

All told, the native Ohioans combined to rack up 539 victories and 5,089 strikeouts.

But despite the similarities, very few people mistook them for one another—although it did happen on one notable occasion.

Longtime San Francisco Giants announcer Hank Greenwald was perched in the Astrodome calling a game when he looked ahead on the schedule. As it turned out, the Giants were slated to face the Astros' Joe Niekro the following evening. However, the Giants' diet of knuckleballs would only increase as their subsequent game would see them squaring off in Atlanta against Phil Niekro.

It was an odd coincidence and something the acerbic Greenwald knew he had to mention to his listening audience.

However, Hank misspoke when he inadvertently said that the

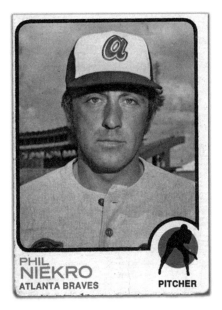

Astros would be sending *Phil* Niekro to the mound and that *Joe* Niekro would be the Braves' pitcher.

Catching his error almost immediately, the witty Greenwald deftly reversed the information before apologetically adding:

"Honestly, folks, all Niekros don't look alike."

Follies Factoids

Phil Niekro is the all-time Atlanta Braves pitching leader in victories, games, innings, and shutouts.

Joe Niekro is the all-time Houston Astros pitching leader in victories.

From 1979-1996, Hank Greenwald broadcast 2,798 consecutive games for the San Francisco Giants and New York Yankees.

Both Joe Niekro and Hank Greenwald had sons who ended up in the San Francisco Giants organization. Doug Greenwald has been announcing games for the Fresno Grizzlies (the Giants' Class AAA affiliate) since 2003. Lance Niekro ended up playing four seasons for the Giants. Was he a knuckleballer? Nope, he was a first baseman.

Although the three Niekros combined to play fifty major league seasons, they only got to play five postseason games among them.

Lance Niekro's 17 career home runs surpassed the aggregate total of 8 that had been hit by his dad and uncle.

Follies Puzzle Clue:

QUESTION: If you were at Turner Field in Atlanta and you had to go to the nearest major league stadium, what city would you depart for?
CLUE: If you answered either Houston or Miami, you would be way off.
(An additional clue appears on page 191)

34

THE ONCE SECRET STRATEGY

n the year 1967, baseball first caught a glimpse into its own future. The St. Louis Cardinals had just taken the World Series. Of course, that's not unusual. Only the Yankees have won more. But back in '67, the Cardinals managed to secure the victory with an unprecedented facet. Their closer, Joe Hoerner, had averaged only 1.16 innings per appearance. In effect, he was a *light saver.* In addition, Joe's teammate, Ron Willis, added 10 saves of his own (and his average stint had taken less than 4 outs as well).

For relief pitchers of that era, these relatively light workloads were highly unusual.

Case in point: In 1966, the two firemen for the World Champion Baltimore Orioles (Stu Miller and Eddie Fisher) logged an aggregate average of 1.72 innings per game.

Had Red Schoendienst's '67 Cardinals discovered a competitive advantage?

Perhaps.

After all, the Cardinals had handily won the NL pennant over the Giants, Cubs, and ten other teams, none of whom had used their closers as sparingly.

The pattern held true in the Fall Classic. The Cardinals had defeated the Red Sox, a club whose top saver (John Wyatt) was used to averaging 1.56 innings per game.

Schoendienst must have liked what he saw because the next season, Joe Hoerner's average stint went all the way down to 1.04 innings. Additionally, his ERA shrank to 1.48 from the 2.59 he had posted the year before. Of course, '68 was a great year for pitchers.

Due to Joe's effectiveness and a few other factors (Bob Gibson, Steve Carlton, Curt Flood, Lou Brock, Orlando Cepeda), the Cardinals easily coasted to their second consecutive pennant.

However, in 1969, Hoerner's workload per game rose and so did his ERA. This development coincided with St. Louis failing to win the pennant.

What team did this house of Cards fall to? Well, they fell to the 1969 Miracle Mets, who had *also* become one of the few teams to begin utilizing a *light saver* (a closer whose average stint is less than 4 outs long).

In all likelihood, a few of baseball's top minds began noticing this emerging trend.

It was in 1970 that a rookie manager named Sparky Anderson took over the reigns of the Cincinnati Reds. His primary saver that year was Wayne Granger, a former teammate of Joe Hoerner.

The year prior to Sparky's arrival, Granger had averaged a hearty 1.61 innings per game out of the pen. But under the eye of Captain Hook, Granger's average stint went all the way down to 1.26.

What success did Cincy reap that year? Their victory total improved by thirteen games, and the Reds won their way into the postseason for only the second time in thirty years.

However, in the 1970 Fall Classic, they fell to Earl Weaver's Baltimore Orioles. It shouldn't go without saying that Weaver had also bucked the conventional wisdom by using a light saver of his own (Pete Richert). Apparently, the lesson of the Miracle Mets had not been lost on Earl either.

What did the future hold for the Cincinnati Reds and Baltimore Orioles?

During the decade of the 1970s, these two franchises combined for eleven playoff berths and finished first and second in total franchise victories.

A coincidence?

Perhaps. Probably. Almost assuredly.

But it sure makes you wonder.

THE ABERRATION

In 1970, Pete Richert of the Orioles became the third *light saver* in four seasons to win a World Series ring.

A new idea as to how managers should utilize closers seemed to be on the verge of exploding throughout the major leagues.

But it didn't.

Although the strategy was a glimpse into the future of baseball, the "light saver" trend reversed almost as fast as it had begun.

For in the 1971 World Series, the Pittsburgh Pirates downed the Orioles, and they reached that pinnacle using Dave Giusti (an old-style closer). In comparison, Earl Weaver's one-two punch of light savers (Eddie Watt and Pete Richert) went home empty handed.

Then, from 1972–1974, a dashing young closer for the Oakland A's won three rings, and he did so while averaging 1.76 innings per appearance. In a sense, the mold had been recast.

Other workhorse closers of that era who became key pieces to a championship puzzle included:

> **Sparky Lyle** (*1.90 innings per stint for the '77 Yankees*)
> **Goose Gossage** (*2.13 IPS for the '78 Yankees*)
> **Kent Tekulve** (*1.43 IPS for the '79 Pirates*)
> **Bruce Sutter** (*1.46 IPS for the '82 Cardinals*)
> **Willie Hernandez** (*1.75 IPS for the '84 Tigers*)
> **Dan Quisenberry** (*1.54 IPS for the '85 Royals*)

In fact, from 1971–1986, only one team managed to win it all with a light saver. That team was the 1981 Los Angeles Dodgers. However, it should be noted that skipper Tommy Lasorda did not utilize his closer (Steve Howe) as a light saver the year before or the year after. So 1981 was an aberration—but so, too, were a lot of things during that unfortunate strike-filled year.

In 1986, Davey Johnson managed the New York Mets to a World Championship.

The Mets' closer was a workhorse named Roger McDowell (1.71 IPS), who not only saved twenty-two regular season games but won an additional fourteen. For good measure, Roger picked up the victory in Game Seven against the Red Sox.

What no one realized at the time was that Roger McDowell would end up being the last of the Mohicans.

In 1987, manager Tom Kelly of the Twins took a page out of the Red Schoendienst / Sparky Anderson playbook and transformed Jeff Reardon into a light saver. At the very least, the move didn't hurt Minnesota. After all, they brought home the trophy that year.

Tom Kelly's successful maneuver opened the floodgates for the new wave of relief specialists who came into fashion, a breed who typically enter a game in the ninth inning without any runners on base.

Some of the great light savers who have also won World Series rings have included:

> **Dennis Eckersley** *(1.13 innings per stint for the '89 A's)*
> **Rick Aguilera** *(1.10 IPS for the '91 Twins)*
> **John Wetteland** *(1.03 IPS for the '96 Yankees)*
> **Robb Nen** *(1.01 IPS for the '97 Marlins)*
> **Mariano Rivera** *(1.11 IPS for the '98, '99 and '00 Yankees)*
> **Troy Percival** *(0.97 IPS for the '02 Angels)*
> **Keith Foulke** *(1.15 IPS for the '04 Red Sox)*
> **Jason Isringhausen** *(0.98 IPS for the '06 Cardinals)*
> **Jonathan Papelbon** *(0.99 IPS for the '07 Red Sox)*
> **Brad Lidge** *(0.96 IPS for the '08 Phillies)*

35

THE PROLIFIC CLOSERS: DECADE BY DECADE

MOST SAVES DURING THE 1950s

Ellis Kinder, BOS	96		Marv Grissom, NYG-SF	58
Clem Labine, BROOK-LAD	82		Ray Narleski, CLE	58
Jim Konstanty, PHI-NYY	65		Hoyt Wilhelm, NYG-SL-CLE	58

Note: Ellis Kinder (mentioned in Chapter 2) was never selected as an all-star.

MOST SAVES DURING THE 1960s

Hoyt Wilhelm, BAL-C	152		Ron Perranoski, LAD-MIN	138
Roy Face, PIT	142		Dick Radatz, BOS	122
Stu Miller, SF-BAL	138			

Note: In 1965, solely in relief, Hoyt Wilhelm tallied 144 innings.

MOST SAVES DURING THE 1970s

Rollie Fingers, OAK-SD	209		Dave Giusti, PIT	140
Sparky Lyle, BOS-NYY	190		Tug McGraw, NYM-PHIL	132
Mike Marshall, MON-LAD-MIN	177			

Note: From 1974 to 77, I was able to notch forty victories and appear in 46% of my team's games—a sign of the times.

MOST SAVES DURING THE 1980s

Jeff Reardon, MON-MIN	264	Goose Gossage, NYY-SD	206
Dan Quisenberry, KC	239	Bruce Sutter, CHC-SL-ATL	195
Lee Smith, CHC-BOS	234		

Note: During the 1980s, Jeff Reardon played in only one All-Star Game.

MOST SAVES DURING THE 1990s

John Wetteland, MON-NYY-TEX	295	Jeff Montgomery, KC	285
Dennis Eckersley, OAK-STL	293	Rick Aguilera, MIN	282
Randy Myers, CIN-SD-CHC-BAL	291		

MOST SAVES FROM 2000 TO 2008

Mariano Rivera, NYY	353	Billy Wagner, HOU-PHIL-NYM	284
Trevor Hoffman, SD	326	Armando Benitez, NYM-FLA-SF	230
Jason Isringhausen, OAK-SL	284		

Note: Mariano Rivera was once John Wetteland's set-up man.

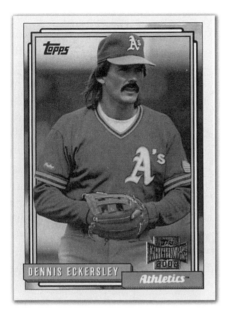

Follies Factoids

The closer with the most career saves among those who didn't crack any of the above lists is John Franco, who saved 424 games for the Reds and Mets from 1984 to 2003.

36

DISCO DEMOLITION NIGHT

◇◇

F or those of you lucky enough to have been born too late, please allow me to briefly explain the phenomenon of disco.

In essence, "disco" was a prehistoric version of techno music, and it somehow inspired all kinds of non-dancers in uncomfortably tight pants to groove the night away. Wailing vocals, violins, harps, drum machines, electric flute solos, inferior moustaches, and a simplistic four-on-the-floor beat were hallmarks of this sickeningly dumb and saccharine art form.

But, though the trend of disco was popular in the mid 1970s, by the end of the decade, the fever started to break—even on Saturday nights.

However, in Chicago, the explosive hatred for this form of quasi-music was about to make baseball history. White Sox owner Bill Veeck was already well known for his wildly creative publicity stunts. After all, he once hired a midget to take a major league at-bat (he walked). On another occasion, Veeck hired a clownish physical comedian as a coach and actually installed him in the coaching box to entertain fans *during* innings. Once, Veeck even let the fans manage a game by holding up placards to display their decisions (they were successful). He even had his team play in shorts for a brief while, which didn't make stealing bases or diving for baseballs a whole lot of fun.

But despite his many eccentricities, Bill Veeck had a knack for knowing how to draw fans to the ballpark—even when his teams weren't winning. As an example, Veeck was the first guy to shoot off fireworks whenever one of his hitters would go yard—but as you might already know, whenever you mess with explosives, they can have a way of backfiring.

The following is the story of Bill Veeck's greatest backfire ever—and as you probably guessed, it involved disco.

July 12, 1979

It seemed like a good idea at the time. To attract additional people to the ballpark, Bill Veeck and his son Mike ran a promotion they called "Disco Demolition Night."

Here's how it was supposed to work: Fans who brought in one of their unwanted disco records would be granted access to the team's twilight double-header for a mere ninety-eight cents. Then, after the first game was in the books, a large crate filled with nearly twenty thousand diabolical discs collected from fans would be brought to center field so that it could be blown to smithereens.

What could go wrong?

At the time, the Chisox's top drawing cards included Chet "The Jet" Lemon and my old teammate Claudell Washington. But even so, the team was only drawing about fifteen thousand fans per game. However, with this ingenious new disco promotion, the Veecks had their fingers crossed that attendance might exceed twenty thousand. They got their wish.

The event was co-promoted by Steve Dahl, a local disc jockey who was already in the habit of blowing up disco records as part of his radio show. Steve's role at the ballpark that evening was simple. He was to walk out to centerfield, wearing an army helmet and dressed in fatigues, where he would then ignite a bomb that would destroy the thousands upon thousands of discs that had been collected. That's entertainment.

But there was a small problem. If anything, the event was promoted too well. More than seventy-five thousand people showed up.

Kids, that's a lot of vinyl! The event at Comiskey Park officially sold out, but that little fact didn't hinder scores of additional people from breaking into the ballpark by climbing their way in—and seemingly everyone, including the trespassers, were packing music. The staff had expected to only collect about twenty thousand records for the stunt, so once they hit that mark, they simply stopped collecting. This meant that nearly fifty-five thousand Frisbee-shaped discs stayed in the hands of the fans during the game.

But things started out fairly okay. The crowd was mostly calm, and there were only a few airborne objects flung around during the first half of the double-header.

In a battle between two fifth-place teams, Sparky Anderson's Tigers took the first game by a score of 4-1. But few people seemed to care because they had come for the half-time show.

Steve Dahl, the triggerman, took to the field. He then rallied the crowd's hatred toward disco music to an even higher point. The thousands in attendance sat on edge waiting for the explosion.

It was a strange and unusual scene. Even through his thick bottle-like glasses, White Sox announcer Harry Carey couldn't help but see that something highly unusual was going on. Numerous people who normally attended rock concerts were aimlessly roaming through the packed sports stadium. Others sat intensely in their seats waiting for the explosion. Marijuana smoke began wafting through the air, mixing with the more familiar smells of beer, peanuts, and hot dogs. The place buzzed with an odd vibe. Try to imagine what would happen if you combined Woodstock with Wrestlemania.

Beer, firecrackers, and black vinyl discs started flying through the air. Mike Veeck watched with ever-whitening knuckles. Although he must have been proud of the massive turnout, he was also worried that things could get out of hand.

Then, it happened.

The disc jockey set off the explosion. KA-BOOM!

The bomb not only destroyed the records, it tore a huge hole in the outfield grass. The crowd roared. Smoke instantly floated up into a cloud of anarchy. The resonance of the bomb incited the crowd into a frenzy, and at that point a lone man in the stands took it upon himself to climb down onto the field.

Mike Veeck would later comment, "The second that first guy shimmied down the outfield wall, I knew my life was over."

Within just a few minutes, thousands of fans stormed the field. Some lit brush fires while others merely raided the dugouts for bats. One fan literally stole second base. Did I mention that they lit brush fires?

Those calmer fans who stayed in the stands started sailing their black Frisbees, which sliced through the air with fury, and sometimes, right into people. Never before has a style of music done so much damage to a populace. The hit disco tune *Staying Alive* by the Bee Gees was never quite so relevant.

Of course, the riot police were called in and eventually Chicago's finest managed to quell the angry, fiery exuberance to a whimper.

As for the White Sox, well, they were forced to forfeit that second game to Detroit. This was a break for the Tigers because there was no way that Sparky was going to bring his team back onto that field.

As for the true White Sox fans in attendance, they were highly disappointed that they didn't get to see the second game of the twin bill. However, they did get a head full of bizarre memories that would last them a lifetime.

… and for ninety-eight cents, that's a bargain in anyone's book.

Follies Factoids

Just twenty-two days after Disco Demolition Night, Tony La Russa made his major league debut as a manager— and he did so for these very same Chicago White Sox.

There have been eighteen men in baseball history that went by the given name of Chet, but not a single one has appeared in the major leagues since the playing days of White Sox star Chet Lemon. Like disco, and the Montreal Expos, the name Chet simply became a vestige of a bygone era.

Catcher Milt May played for both the '79 Tigers and the '79 White Sox. Milt May also holds the distinction for having driven in the 1,000,000th run in baseball history.

THE
BILL "SPACEMAN" LEE
DOSSIER

LEE, Bill
DOSSIER - 37

EARLY CHILDHOOD: Both Southern and Northern California

BOYHOOD FACT: Was eleven years old when the Dodgers moved to Los Angeles, instantly making him a fan

LINEAGE: Grandfather played for a Pacific Coast League team; Aunt pitched a no-hitter for the ladies' league that was popularized in the film A League of Their Own

COLLEGE: University of Southern California

OTHER PLAYERS WHO PLAYED FOR USC IN THE 1960s: Jim Barr, Dave Kingman, Marcel Lacheman, Rene Lacheman, Tom Seaver

COLLEGE TRIVIA: Al Campanis of the Dodgers told Lee that he didn't possess the requisite stuff to make the majors

DRAFTED: Was the 507th pick in the 1968 draft

QUOTE: People are too hung up on winning. I can get off on a really good helmet throw.

LEE, Bill   DOSSIER - 37

PLAYERS DRAFTED AHEAD OF HIM IN THE '68 DRAFT:
Thurman Munson, Bill Buckner, Greg Luzinski, Gary
Matthews, Doyle Alexander, Steve Stone, Burt Hooten,
Chris Speier, Oscar Gamble, Al Bumbry, Ben Oglivie,
Cecil Cooper, Bobby Valentine, and Tom Kelly

MINOR LEAGUE GAMES BEFORE DEBUT: 26

MOST FREQUENT MINOR LEAGUE HOME:
Pittsfield, Massachusetts

MINOR LEAGUE TRIVIA: Posted an overall 1.81 earned
run average

DEBUT YEAR: 1969

EARLIEST TEAMMATES INCLUDED: Carl Yastrzemski,
Reggie Smith, Rico Petrocelli, Sparky Lyle

AGE AT DEBUT: 22

FINAL YEAR: 1982

FINAL TEAMMATES INCLUDED: Andre Dawson,
Gary Carter, Terry Francona, Tim Raines,
Jeff Reardon, Chris Speier

HIS STANCE ON DOUBLE-HEADERS, GREENPEACE, and
POPULATION CONTROL: Pro

LEE, Bill

DOSSIER - 37

HIS STANCE ON THE DESIGNATED HITTER, ASTROTURF, and POLYESTER UNIFORMS: Con

ROLE:
Starter - 54%
Middler - 35%
Closer - 11%

PRIMARY CATCHER: Carlton Fisk

TOTAL MANAGERS PLAYED FOR: 6

PRIMARY MANAGER: Eddie Kasko

MAJOR LEAGUE AFFILIATIONS:
- Boston Red Sox (77%)
- Montreal Expos (23%)

TOTAL SEASONS IN THE MAJOR LEAGUES: 14

NUMBER OF SEASONS ON A LOSING TEAM: 0

CAREER STATS: 119-90/3.62 ERA/713 K/19 saves

BEST SEASON: 1973 (17-11/2.75 ERA)

CAREER FIELDING RECORD: .947

LEE, Bill

DOSSIER - 37

CAREER HITTING STATS: .208/2 HR/10 RBI

INJURY OR REST RATE: 21%

PLAYOFF RECORD:
2 postseasons - 4 games
1-2 2.93 ERA 8 K
1 pennant

ALL-STAR TEAMS: 1

ALL-STAR STATS: Did not play

MOST FREQUENT FOE:
Graig Nettles - 87 plate appearances
(.260 BA/2 HR/13 RBI)

MOST FREQUENT CRITIC: Red Sox manager Don Zimmer,
who Lee christened "The Designated Gerbil"

ANOTHER SPACEMAN QUOTE: Most of the managers are
lifetime .220 hitters. For years, pitchers have been
getting these guys out 75 percent of the time and
that's why they don't like us.

THE HITTER HE OWNED:
Ed Brinkman: .184 (9 for 49) with 1 HR, 4 RBIs,
0 walks, and 8 strikeouts

LEE, Bill

DOSSIER - 37

THE HITTER WHO OWNED HIM:
Amos Otis: .373 (19 for 51) with 4 HRs, 13 RBIs, 5 walks,
and 1 strikeout

THE HITTER SPACEMAN STRUCK OUT MOST OFTEN:
Reggie Jackson (12)

ANOTHER QUOTE FROM THE SPACEMAN: Baseball is the
belly button of our society. Straighten out baseball
and you straighten out the rest of the world.

HIS RECORD AGAINST HALL OF FAMERS:
376 AT-BATS (.277 BA/11 HR/49 RBI/51 WALKS/39K)

OTHER BASEBALL EXPERIENCE: Pitched for the Alaska
Goldpanners during their midnight sun game in 1967.
In 2008, pitched for the senior league. Also pitched
for Oil Can Boyd's Traveling All-Stars

HOME AWAY FROM HOME: Comiskey Park (Chicago)
(5-0/2.94 ERA/2 saves)

BEHAVIORS: talked to animals, was once fined $250
for sprinkling marijuana on his pancakes, did yoga
and yogurt

MOST FREQUENT OPPONENT: Detroit Tigers

LEE, Bill

CLOSEST STATISTICAL TWIN: Larry Gura   DOSSIER - 37

HALL OF FAME CALIBER RATING: 43%

ANOTHER SPACEMAN QUOTE: I believed in drug
testing a long time ago. All through the sixties
I tested everything.

POLITICAL CAREER: In 1988, ran for President of
the United States as the nominee for the Canadian
Political Rhinoceros Party

POLITICAL SLOGAN: No guns. No butter. Both can kill.

POLITICAL OUTCOME: Lost the election to George H.W.
Bush by several million votes

INDUCTION INTO THE RED SOX HALL OF FAME: 2008

38

SAUSAGES AND PRESIDENTS

◇◇

The origins of sausage racing are cloaked in mystery. However, experts on the subject agree that it probably began in Milwaukee around 1993. The more maverick thinkers suggest that the first live-action sausage race may have been part of a primitive ceremony to honor an ancient legend (Robin Yount) on the occasion of his uniform number being retired.

We should all be so honored.

The original ritual was quite simple and normal for its culture.

A large bratwurst, wearing Bavarian lederhosen and nearing eight feet in height, would line up in preparation to run.

Next to him at the starting block would be a large Italian sausage (wearing a chef's hat) that answered to the name *Guido*. I think we can all agree that this particular sausage was refreshing for its complete avoidance of ethnic stereotype.

Finally, there was Stosh Jonjak—a Polish sausage who wore a rugby shirt and dark sunglasses. Thankfully, this third contestant wasn't from Japan; otherwise, veterans of World War II may have had a really hard time finding a meat to root for.

What began as a minor amusement soon grew in both prestige and stature. Eventually, both an All-American hot dog and a sombrero-clad Mexican chorizo joined in on the sausage-fest.

Weiner take all!

But the expansion didn't stop there.

In 2006, the Washington Nationals resurrected the four icons of Mount Rushmore for the purpose of having them run their own little competitive wind sprint.

But unlike in Milwaukee, their race has always featured a perennial loser...Teddy Roosevelt. Although a seasoned racer, after three years, Teddy has yet to win a single contest. Some attribute this ineptitude to the fact that he had asthma as a child. Others feel the malaria he contracted in South America is the primary cause. Other analysts simply cite the overall superior athleticism of Jefferson, Lincoln, and Washington. After all, that trio managed to also trump Teddy by having better memorials.

In a way, it's sad to see Teddy lose each and every race he enters. Although he was once renowned for his courage and candor, in modern times, he has sadly become known both for his unsportsmanlike conduct and for taking short cuts, literally.

On occasions, Teddy seemed to finish in first place, but he was disqualified every time for cheating. He once got the boot for using a dune buggy to motor past the others. Another time, TR enlisted the aid of a rickshaw, and on yet another occasion, he utilized a zip line. Well, he always was a fan of extreme sports.

As for those famous sausage races in Miltown that inspired the running of the presidents, they have had their fair share of controversy as well…but none more than when the Pittsburgh Pirates came to town on July 9, 2003.

On that day, as the five bloated meat casings made their way past the Pirate dugout, first baseman Randall Simon grabbed a bat and lightly swung at the head of Guido the Italian sausage. Of course, he connected. After all, he is a professional hitter.

It was a funny visual, but the velocity was sufficient that it not only knocked Guido to the ground, but caused the falling Italian sausage to take down the All-American hot dog (Frankie Furter) as well. Instantly, it was one of those classic "oops" moments.

But there was a silver lining to all of this. In an act of unprecedented sportsmanship within the world of meat racing, the Polish sausage stopped running. Why? Well, it was to help up his fallen comrades. He may even have given the Pirate slugger a stern looking at for having caused such problems. As for Randall Simon, he was actually arrested for the incident, suspended by Major League Baseball for three games, and had to pay a fine.

But all's well that ends well because Guido didn't declare a vendetta; nor did he sanction a mob hit in retaliation. Randall made personal amends by not only apologizing, but also by granting the Italian sausage's request to have the offending bat autographed.

The incident became a rallying cry of sorts for Brewer fans everywhere as in almost no time, T-shirts began popping up all over Miller Park spouting the catch phrase *Don't Whack Our Weiner*.

39

AN ODD BUT MODEST PROPOSAL

Until now, the chapters of this book were written under the best of circumstances. When these words were entered into a keyboard, all was sober, comfy, and quiet within the writing rooms, except for perhaps the sound of typing and the din of baseball games being broadcast in the background.

But for this chapter, the rules were changed. This entry was entirely conceived and written by Yellowstone Ritter while he was on a cross-country flight across America. He was seated in a row in front of a family with both a wailing infant and a toddler who kicked like a Rockette.

As for Yellowstone's own row on the plane, he had the middle seat and fate had placed him between two passengers so large he expected them to start throwing around ceremonial salt. To add to the difficulties, Yellowstone boarded the plane three sheets to the wind, and then ordered four mini-bottles of whiskey until the flight attendant cut him off for fear he was damaging his liver.

So now, without more adieu, I present a proposal from a man (with a whiskey-soaked brain) about how he would make the national pastime even better.

BASEBALL IS A WONDERFULLY FAIR GAME.

The umpires are impartial, the losing team gets just as many outs as the winning team, and even in a dinosaur bone yard like Coors Field, which I just looked down and saw through my window, each team must play each other in the same ballpark, no matter what its odd dimensions.

But despite these many equalities, I sometimes wonder if some teams just don't have wildly unfair advantages over others.

For example, let's compare what the Cincinnati Reds must deal with as compared to the Texas Rangers.

The Reds must compete with FIVE other teams for a division title whereas the Rangers must compete with only THREE.

Of course, there is the wild-card playoff berth that helps assuage the pain of the also-rans, but once again, the Rangers have an advantage over the Reds. After all, Texas needs to merely beat out TEN other teams to get that wild-card spot, whereas the Reds must beat out TWELVE.

Then, there's the schedule, which isn't set down in any sort of true round-robin formation. Wow, that seventh whiskey kicked in.

I am truly flying in every sense of the word. Thank goodness for spellcheck, otherwise I'd be mispelling words all over the place.

Anyhooziewhatsit, let's compare what the New York Mets and the Florida Marlins (two interdivisional rivals) have to deal with.

During interleague play, the Mets consistently draw a home-and-away series against the powerhouse Yankees, whereas the Marlins draw the Rays, a team that until 2008 had significantly less firepower than the Bombers.

So, due to these and other disadvantages, I propose that once every ten years (let's say in those years that end with a five), baseball should institute an "EQUALIZE YEAR."

During this season, Major League Baseball would change things around so the teams that usually catch the breaks have to switch places with the teams that usually do not.

The schedules would be designed so that the teams that had been forced to play against tougher-than-average competition would have to carry a lighter load. In addition, for this one bizarre season, teams that have significant payroll advantages over others would have to play more often against one another.

Oh, I'm now flying over Kansas. It sure is pretty—not a Starbucks in sight!!

Now, for this anomaly year, we would need to redraw divisional lines. I propose we temporarily transfer three teams from the AL Central to the AL West, and then also swap five AL teams with five NL teams.

During this "EQ year," both the AL Central and NL Central would only have four teams in their ranks. All other teams (except for the suddenly bloated NL West) would have five. I just ordered a Drambuie because the plane ran out of my brand of whiskey. You all know what that means: that my best ideas are now ahead of us.

So, I'm thinking that this EQ year could prove to be incredibly interesting. General managers of certain teams would need to plan for the eventuality that they will either soon have to have their pitchers hit, or they will need to start scouting for someone to fill an extended designated hitter role. Of course, many will complain that it could cause injury to AL pitchers if they suddenly had to hit, but it's not like that common complaint has *ever* kept a NL team from trading for a C.C. Sabathia, Rich Harden, or a Joe Blanton.

Now, I think I should get started in drawing the divisional lines. I also think I just flew over Nebraska. Nice. That big building down below is either a Cabela's sporting goods emporium or an airport hangar. No, it's too big to merely house airplanes—it must be a Cabela's.

One could argue that there would be no need for interleague play this particular year, but I would have it anyway—to help match up teams who are of a similar caliber and also to equalize the inequities of past scheduling. Besides, it would be a shame if the Cubs and Cardinals (and other natural rivals like the Rangers and Astros) went an entire year without clashing.

Without adieu that is further, I now present the new divisions for this initial "EQ year." As an added benefit, imagine all the travel time, jet lag, and jet fuel that this realignment would allow baseball to cut down on.

THE TEMPORARY DIVISIONAL REALIGNMENTS FOR THE EQ YEAR

The American League

East Division	Central Division	West Division
ATLANTA BRAVES	CHICAGO CUBS	DETROIT TIGERS
BOSTON RED SOX	CHICAGO WHITE SOX	KANSAS CITY ROYALS
NEW YORK METS	CINCINNATI REDS	MINNESOTA TWINS
NEW YORK YANKEES	CLEVELAND INDIANS	SEATTLE MARINERS
PHILADELPHIA PHILLIES		TEXAS RANGERS

NOTES:

1. Switching to the AL West would be a homecoming of sorts for both the Kansas City Royals and the Minnesota Twins.
2. One wonders if the Mets–Yankees and Cubs–White Sox matchups would take on a similar dynamic to the legendary rivalry between the Brooklyn Dodgers and the New York Giants.
3. It's odd to see the Detroit Tigers in a Western Division, but back in the nineteenth century—it was entirely fitting. In fact, one of Detroit's earliest nicknames was "The Paris of the West."

The National League

East Division	Central Division	West Division
BALTIMORE ORIOLES	HOUSTON ASTROS	ARIZONA DIAMONDBACKS
FLORIDA MARLINS	MILWAUKEE BREWERS	COLORADO ROCKIES
TAMPA BAY RAYS	PITTSBURGH PIRATES	LOS ANGELES ANGELS
TORONTO BLUE JAYS	ST. LOUIS CARDINALS	LOS ANGELES DODGERS
WASHINGTON NATIONALS		OAKLAND A's
		SAN DIEGO PADRES
		SAN FRANCISCO GIANTS

NOTES:

1. The Diamondbacks, Rockies, Dodgers, Padres, and Giants wouldn't be thrilled with this realignment, but in future "EQ years" they could all be placed in four-team divisions to offset the imbalance.
2. Short of building two new stadiums, a Rays–Marlins interdivisional rivalry might be the next best thing toward boosting attendance in Florida.
3. Perhaps the A's–Giants, Angels–Dodgers, and Nationals–Orioles would all develop fierce rivalries over the course of this one special season, especially since they would be playing more than six games.

(FOR GEEKS ONLY)

(please skip this page unless you're really into math)

The schedules during an EQ year could be designed as follows:

AL East: 22 games against each team in their own division
6 games against all other teams in the American League
4 games against every team in the NL East

AL Central: 26 games against each team in their own division
6 games against all other teams in the American League
6 games against every team in the NL Central

AL West: 22 games against each team in their own division
6 games against all other teams in the American League
2–4 games against every team in the NL West
(Four of the AL West teams would play (6) three-game match-ups and (1)two-game matchup against the NL West teams; the fifth AL West team would have (4) three-game matchups and (4) two-game matchups against the NL West teams.)

NL East: 19 games against each team in their own division
6 games against all other teams in the National League
4 games against every team in the AL East

NL Central: 22 games against each team in their own division
6 games against all other teams in the National League
6 games against every team in the AL Central

NL West: 15–18 games against the teams in their own division
2–4 games against every team in the AL West *(Six of the NL West teams would play (4) three-game matchups and (1) two-game matchup against the AL West teams; the seventh NL West team would have (4) three-game matchups and (2) two-game matchups against the AL West teams.)*

Oh hey, my plane is flying over Lake Michigan. Cool!! Is that the plane shaking or me? I probably shouldn't have had that last shot of Drambuie...

40

THE PIONEER ERA

A TIMELINE OF BASEBALL'S EVOLUTION
THROUGH 1900

1085   "Stool Ball," a primitive stick-and-ball game, is referenced in the Domesday Book, a literary device commissioned by William the Conqueror to better assess the land and resources of England.

1744   Another British book not only mentions "baseball" by name, but also differentiates it from the similar activity of rounders.

c. 1766   "Bat and Ball" becomes popular among children in the American colonies.

1778   American soldiers at Valley Forge pass time by playing "base."

1787   Princeton bans the unruly and undignified game of "baste ball" from its campus.

c. 1798   Author Jane Austen describes her fourteen-year-old heroine in the novel *Northanger Abbey* as preferring "base-ball" to books.

1806   Meriwether Lewis and William Clark attempt to teach the "game of base" to Native Americans.

1820s   Distinct variations of baseball become more popular in New York, New England, Philadelphia, and Canada. Most of them allow "soaking," a method for eliminating base runners by simply beaning them with the ball. In addition, the concept of "foul territory" is alien because defensive players other than the catcher are regularly positioned behind the "striker." Quite often, there's no limit to the amount of players on the field or within a lineup.

1838   The first recorded baseball game takes place in Beechwood, Ontario. This early variation on the game has five bases, which were spaced sixty-three feet apart. Quite unusual for its era, the organizers use foul lines, which create "out-of-bounds" areas.

1842   A social group of well-to-do men begins meeting at a field in Manhattan to regularly play baseball.

1845   This Manhattan group forms a committee (headed by Alexander Cartwright) to decide firm rules. These eventual bylaws call for four bases aligned in a perfect square (forty-two paces apart), for there to be three strikes to an out, and for there to be three outs to a half-inning. These contests are won by whichever team manages to score 21 aces (runs) first, as long as each team gets an equal amount of hands (innings). Unlike the Massachusetts variation of the game, this New York version is "pitched" underhanded and hitters can be called out if the ball they put into play is caught on one bounce. Additionally, the New York game uses a baseball similar to the one used today, whereas the Massachusetts game employs a significantly smaller and denser ball.

1846   The first recorded baseball game in United States history takes place in Hoboken, New Jersey, just across the Hudson River from Manhattan.

c. 1854   Despite its origins among wealthy young men, organized baseball becomes popular with working-class Americans and also develops into something of a spectator sport, especially in Brooklyn.

1857	At a baseball convention in New York, the game's rules become even more formalized. It is decided that games should be a uniform nine innings, that bases should be ninety feet apart (a major reduction from the nearly 126 feet they were at), and that the pitcher should be forty-five feet away from the hitter. (Previously, they could pitch from almost anywhere.)
1858	Umpires begin to call strikes on hitters who take pitches. Up to that point, taking lots of pitches had been a tactic to both allow more base stealing and to tire out the opposing hurler.
1859	The first championship in baseball history is decided.
1861 –1865	During the Civil War, many Midwestern soldiers pick up the game from their Eastern counterparts. In addition, captured Northerners indirectly teach baseball to Southern soldiers while interred in the Confederate prison camps.
1862	The first enclosed baseball facility, Union Grounds, opens for business in Brooklyn.
c.1860s	During a barnstorming trip to New England, the "New York" version of baseball begins to win over the fans of the Massachusetts version.
1863	Strike zones appear. The pitcher's box also appears, which curbs the running starts that pitchers sometimes used.
1869	The Cincinnati Red Stockings become the first fully professional team.
1871	The first truly professional league, the National Association, is formed.
1872	The regulation size and weight of a baseball as it is known today is firmly decided.
1875	A player is first documented wearing a glove; which at the time was little more than thin leather sheaths with the fingertips cut out (to better control throwing back to the infield). Gloves at the time are thought of as prissy, but within twenty years, they will become standard issue. After five seasons, the National Association disbands in the wake of the formation of a new and improved league that will absorb six of the National Association's franchises.

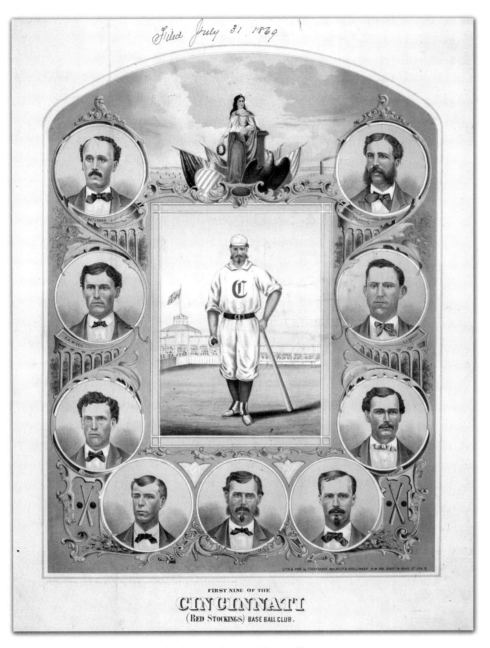

The first professional baseball team

1876   The National League, made up of eight teams, officially begins. Boston, Chicago, Cincinnati, New York, Philadelphia, and St. Louis are among its premiere cities.

1877   The National League expels two teams for missing road games (to save money), and the league constricts to only six teams.

1878   Major League Baseball debuts in Milwaukee.

1879   The National League expands to eight teams.
        Cleveland debuts in this new league.
        Walks are granted to batters whenever the pitcher throws nine balls outside the strike zone.

1880   The requirement needed for a walk is lowered to eight.

1881   Major League Baseball debuts in Detroit.

1883   The requirement needed for a base on balls is lowered to six.

1884   Overhand pitching is allowed and hurlers often request dirt to be built up in the pitching boxes to give them a height advantage.
        The regular season schedule expands past one hundred games for the first time.

1885   Catchers and umpires begin wearing chest protectors.
        In the state of New York, the first African-American team is formed.

1886   Major league baseball debuts in Kansas City.
        Washington, D.C., joins the National League.

1887   Major League Baseball debuts in Pittsburgh.
        The requirement for a base on balls is lowered to five balls.
        A new rule dictates that any batter hit by a pitch gets awarded first base.

1889   Four balls become a walk for the first time.

1890   After a name change, the Philadelphia Phillies officially begin play.

1891   After a name change, the Pittsburgh Pirates officially begin play.
        Major League Baseball attracts one million fans for the first time.

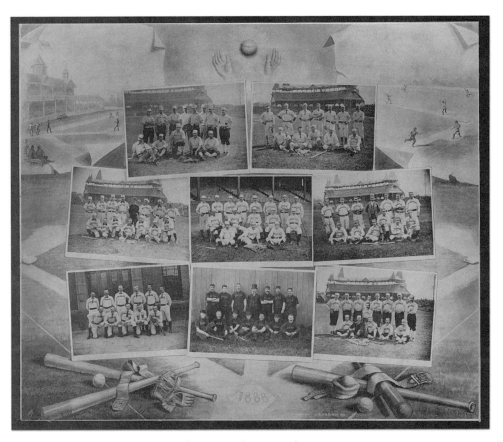

The National League of 1888

1892   The league expands from eight to twelve teams.
        Baltimore joins the new league.
        For the first time, a team plays 150 games.
1893   Pitchers are moved back to 60.5 feet from home plate.
        A pitching rubber is instituted.
        Major League Baseball attracts two million fans for the
        first time.
1895   Babe Ruth is born. The infield fly rule is instituted.
1900   The National League constricts from twelve to eight teams.
        After a name change, the St. Louis Cardinals begin play.

⇥ The All Nineteenth-Century Team ⇤

**Can you imagine meeting up with a group of baseball fans
from the year 1900? Which players would they rave about?
Who were their heroes?**

If you guessed that Ty Cobb, Walter Johnson, and Babe Ruth were among
them, you're way off base. Those guys hadn't come into the spotlight yet.
We've put together a squad consisting of perhaps the twenty-five greatest
players from that era—names that nineteenth-century fans would know well,
even if most are forgotten except by fans who know their baseball history.

All of these pioneering icons had to meet two specific criteria:
1) they had to be enshrined in Cooperstown and
2) the majority of their playing careers had to take place prior to the
beginning of the twentieth century.

-WE NOW PRESENT-

PITCHING STAFF

*(Career statistics for many of the century's premiere hurlers,
along with the franchise they primarily played for)*

	Won-Loss	ERA	Strikeouts
Al Spalding (*Boston Red Stockings*)	253-65	2.14	142
Kid Nichols (*Beaneaters*)	361-208	2.95	1,868
John "Monte" Ward (*Grays*)	164-102	2.10	920
"Smiling" Tim Keefe (*Giants*)	342-225	2.62	2,562
Charley Radbourne (*Grays*)	309-195	2.67	1,830
Pud Galvin (*Bisons*)	364-310	2.86	1,806
John Clarkson (*Beaneaters*)	328-178	2.81	1,978
Mickey Welch (*Giants*)	307-210	2.71	1,850
Amos Rusie (*Giants*)	245-174	3.07	1,934

POSITION PLAYERS

Position		AVG	HR	RBI	SB
C	King Kelly *(White Stockings)*	.308	69	950	368
1B	Cap Anson *(White Stockings)*	.333	97	2,076	276
2B	Bid McPhee *(Reds)*	.271	53	1,067	568
SS	John "Monte" Ward *(Giants)*	.275	26	867	540
3B	George Davis *(Giants)*	.295	73	1,437	616
LF	Jesse "Crab" Burkett *(Spiders)*	.338	75	952	389
CF	Ed Delahanty *(Phillies)*	.346	101	1,464	455
RF	"Orator" Jim O'Rourke *(Giants)*	.311	62	1,203	224

RESERVES

Position		AVG	HR	RBI	SB
C	Buck Ewing *(Giants)*	.303	71	883	354
1B	Roger Connor *(Giants)*	.317	138	1,322	244
1B	Jake "Eagle Eye" Beckley *(Pirates)*	.308	86	1,575	315
2B	Tommy McCarthy *(Beaneaters)*	.292	44	735	468
3B	George Davis *(Giants)*	.295	73	1,437	616
3B	"Big" Dan Brouthers *(Bisons)*	.342	106	1,296	256
LF	Jesse "Crab" Burkett *(Spiders)*	.338	75	952	389
LF	Joe Kelley *(Orioles)*	.317	65	1,194	443
CF	"Sir" Hugh Duffy *(Beaneaters)*	.324	106	1,302	574
CF	"Sliding" Billy Hamilton *(Phillies)*	.344	40	736	912
RF	"Big" Sam Thompson *(Phillies)*	.331	127	1,299	229

Players of the era often played more than one position:

King Kelly was primarily a right fielder.

George Davis was most often a shortstop.

Dan Brouthers was mostly a first baseman.

John Ward is listed as both a pitcher and a shortstop.

Ed Delahanty and Jim O'Rourke were better known as left fielders.

~ Four Of The Greatest

CAP ANSON

★ Legendary Chicago first baseman

★ An RBI machine who amassed a .333 lifetime average

★ Played twenty-seven seasons, finishing with 3,418 hits

★ Played on six pennant winners, five of which he managed

★ Comparable lifetime stats to Paul Molitor

★ A major celebrity of his era

"BIG" ED DELAHANTY

★ Philadelphia Phillies left fielder famous for his speed

★ Once hit 4 home runs in a game

★ In sixteen seasons, compiled a .346 batting average

★ At various points, he led the league in hitting, home runs, RBIs, and stolen bases

★ Shortly after his final game at the age of thirty-five, he tragically plunged over Niagara Falls

Players From This Era ~

"SMILING" TIM KEEFE

★ Submarine pitcher best known for leading the New York Giants to two consecutive championships

★ In thirteen seasons, Keefe compiled 342 victories with a 2.42 ERA

★ Retired with 2,533 strikeouts, a record at that time

★ Comparable lifetime stats to Steve Carlton

JOHN "MONTE" WARD

★ Shortstop on the New York Giants' two championship teams

★ Played seventeen seasons overall, in seven of which he performed double duty as a pitcher

★ Finished with 2,104 hits, 540 stolen bases, 164 victories, and a 2.10 ERA

★ Was also a player-manager for seven seasons

★ A strong advocate for player rights; the Curt Flood of his era

THE DOGHOUSE

Although they were never teammates, early legends Cap Anson and Big Ed Delahanty crossed paths often from 1888 to 1897 as competitors. But the most memorable time they ever connected occurred in Philly in July of 1892.

Delahanty's Quakers were hosting Anson's Chicago White Stockings. Back in that era, baseball fields sometimes featured obstructions, whether it was a flagpole, stray mitts, or even small weatherproof sheds used to store equipment.

With Anson hitting late in the game, he sent a towering shot to center that Delahanty was forced to look up at. However, the ball hit a pole and then bounced down directly into a doghouse-sized container used to store scoreboard panels. However, this was no automatic home run as the doghouse was situated in fair territory.

Anson motored around first base as Delahanty reached down into the large container in hope of finding the horsehide. Unable to locate it, Big Ed himself crawled down inside; how very proactive of him. Unfortunately, Big Ed got wedged like a lemon and couldn't free himself.

By the time a fellow outfielder managed to help him out of the trap, Anson had successfully crossed home plate. Although Big Ed managed to literally escape from the doghouse, he never managed to do so metaphorically.

TEMPORARILY MAJOR LEAGUE

The seventeen major league cities of the nineteenth century that didn't get to host major league franchises in the twentieth century:

Altoona, PA	Providence, RI
Columbus, OH	Richmond, VA
Elizabeth, NJ	Rockford, IL
Fort Wayne, IN	Syracuse, NY
Hartford, CT	Toledo, OH
Keokuk, IA	Troy, NY
Louisville, KY	Wilmington, DE
Middletown, CT	Worcester, MA
New Haven, CT	

NOTABLE DIFFERENCES BETWEEN THE 1900 ST. LOUIS CARDINALS AND THE 2000 ST. LOUIS CARDINALS

~ One team played 142 games; the other played 162 games ~

~ One played at Robison Field; the other played in Busch Stadium ~

~ One's home field could accommodate 15,200 fans;
the other's home field could hold 49,676 ~

~ One team attracted 270,000 fans; the other drew 3,336,493 ~

~ One had outfield dimensions of 470-500-330 with chutes 625 feet away from home plate; the other's had dimensions of 330-402-330 with power alleys 372 feet away ~

~ One's backstop was 120 feet behind home plate; the other's was fifty feet away ~

~ One team used twenty-six players over the course of the year;
the other used forty-six players~

~ One team had five regulars hit .300 or better; the other had only two regulars do so ~

~ One team had an eight-man pitching staff (three starters, three spot starters, one reliever, and one guy up for a cup of coffee); the other used a twenty-four-man staff (five starters, one spot starter, twelve relievers, and six guys up for coffee) ~

~ One team had an average age of twenty-nine; the other's was thirty.
One team hit twice as many triples as home runs; the other team hit nine times as many homers as they did triples ~

~ One team scored an average of 5.23 runs per game;
the other scored an average of 5.48 ~

~ One team surrendered 5.27 runs per game; the other gave up an average of 4.76 ~

~ One team had an ERA of 3.75; the other had an ERA of 4.38 ~

~ One team committed 331 fielding errors; the other only made 111 ~

~ One team knocked out 36 homers, walked 406 times, and struck out on 318 occasions; the other team hit 235 homers, walked 675 times, and struck out on 1,235 occasions ~

~ One team had a guy who hit 15 home runs (Jesse Burkett);
the other team had a guy who hit 42 (Jim Edmonds) ~

~ One team stole 243 bases; the other team swiped 87 ~

~ One pitching staff had three pitchers exceed 282 innings;
the other staff had five pitchers exceed 162 innings ~

~ One team didn't have a single pitcher collect a save;
the other team had a closer save twenty-nine games ~

~ One team's pitching staff hit .196 with 104 hits;
the other staff hit .142 with 48 hits ~

~ One team had a nineteen-game winner (Cy Young);
the other had a twenty-game winner (Darryl Kile) ~

THE THREE ADDITIONAL NINETEENTH-CENTURY PLAYERS WHO ARE ENSHRINED IN COOPERSTOWN

CANDY CUMMINGS
★ Innovative pitcher from the thriving Brooklyn baseball scene in the 1860s and 1870s
★ Credited with inventing the curveball after watching the movement sea shells made when thrown
★ Perhaps the only Hall of Famer who shares the same name as a famous adult film star

FRANK GRANT
★ Known primarily as a powerful but acrobatic second baseman for Buffalo
★ Played integrated minor league baseball with white players before the color barrier was instituted
★ Became the earliest legend from the Negro Leagues inducted into the Hall of Fame

GEORGE WRIGHT
★ Shortstop for the first professional team in history (the 1869 Cincinnati Red Stockings)
★ Arguably, the best hitter, fielder, and base runner of the late 1860s and 1870s
★ In 1876, he became the first hitter in National League history
★ Later in life, he became an innovative sporting goods businessman who helped modernize golf, tennis, and hockey equipment

THE NINETEENTH-CENTURY INNOVATORS ENSHRINED IN COOPERSTOWN

MORGAN BULKELEY
★ First president of the National League
★ Cracked down on illegal gambling
★ Curbed drinking and fan rowdiness at games

ALEXANDER CARTWRIGHT
★ Credited with inventing the modern version of baseball
★ Organized many of the sport's earliest competitions
★ Established the concepts of foul territory, three outs per inning, nine innings per game, nine players per team, and ninety feet between bases.
★ Introduced baseball to California

HENRY CHADWICK

★ Author of baseball's first rule book
★ Inventor of the box score
★ Championed the concept of extra innings
★ Inventor of the "batting average" and "earned run average"

WILLIAM HULBERT

★ Cofounder and second president of the National League
★ Created an impartial central committee to both design schedules and hire umpires
★ Curbed prolific player-jumping by instituting a reserve clause

THE THREE NINETEENTH-CENTURY MANAGERS IN THE HALL OF FAME (NOT NAMED CAP ANSON)

NED HANLON

★ Won three pennants with the Baltimore Orioles and another two with the Brooklyn Superbas
★ Over the course of his nineteen-year career, he also was a mainstay in both Pittsburgh and Cincinnati
★ Overall, finished with 1,313 wins and a .530 winning permillage
★ Aggressive tactician who favored both the "hit and run"and a hitting technique called the Baltimore Chop (swinging downward on the ball to cause a high bounce that takes extensive time to field properly)

FRANK SELEE

★ Won five pennants during his twelve seasons as manager of the Boston Beaneaters. Finished his managing career with a four-year stint with the Chicago Orphans/Cubs
★ He finished with 1,284 wins and a .598 winning permillage
★ Was an exceptional talent evaluator

HARRY WRIGHT

★ Won four National Association pennants as manager for the Boston Red Stockings and another two pennants after they joined the National League as the Boston Red Caps
★ Was player-manager for all but one of these championship seasons
★ Besides his eleven years at the helm in Boston, he spent two years managing the Providence Greys and another eleven managing the Philadelphia Quakers/Phillies
★ Wright ended up with 1,225 wins and a .581 winning permillage
★ The first to utilize defensive shifts to counteract certain hitters
★ First to have defenders back one another up

THE PRIMARY NINETEENTH-CENTURY BALL CLUBS (1871-1900)

★ Boston Red Stockings/Red Caps/Beaneaters ~ *30 seasons*
★ Chicago White Stockings/Colts/Orphans ~ *28 seasons*
★ Cincinnati Red Stockings/Reds (two versions) ~ *24 seasons*
★ St. Louis Brown Stockings/Browns/Perfectos/Cardinals (three versions) ~ *22 seasons*
★ Brooklyn Atlantics/Grays/Grooms/Bridegrooms/Superbas ~ *21 seasons*
★ Pittsburgh Alleghenys/Pirates ~ *19 seasons*
★ Baltimore Orioles ~ *18 seasons*
★ Louisville Eclipse/Colonels ~ *18 seasons*
★ New York Gothams/Giants ~ *18 seasons*
★ Philadelphia Quakers/Phillies ~ *18 seasons*
★ Philadelphia Athletics (four versions) ~ *17 seasons*
★ Cleveland Spiders ~ *13 seasons*
★ Buffalo Bisons (two versions) ~ *8 seasons*
★ Detroit Wolverines ~ *8 seasons*
★ Providence Grays ~ *8 seasons*
★ Washington Senators ~ *8 seasons*
★ Cleveland Blues ~ *8 seasons*
★ New York Mutuals ~ *8 seasons*

THE FOUR MOST DOMINANT BALL CLUBS OF THE NINETEENTH CENTURY (1871–1900)

Boston Red Stockings/Red Caps/Beaneaters
★ the ancestors of today's Atlanta Braves
★ 10 championships

Chicago White Stockings
★ the ancestors of today's Chicago Cubs
★ 6 championships

Baltimore Orioles
★ no direct lineage to any modern team
★ 3 championships

Brooklyn Bridegrooms/Superbas
★ the ancestors of today's Los Angeles Dodgers
★ 3 championships

The Boston Beaneaters playing at South End Grounds

41

THE TOUGH LUCK OF DON SUTTON

◇◇

Hall of Famer Don Sutton pitched for the Los Angeles Dodgers from 1966 through 1980. However, the Dodgers failed to win a single World Series during this fifteen-season stretch. However, they won it all the year before Don's debut (1965) and also took home the big trophy the year after he left (1981).

★   ★   ★   ★   ★

Sutton ended up pitching for the Dodgers again in 1988 (before calling it a career in August of that season). Somehow, with Don no longer aboard, the Dodgers went on to win the Fall Classic that year as well.

★   ★   ★   ★   ★

Don Sutton, despite pitching nine seasons for other ball clubs, is the all-time victory leader in Dodger franchise history (a feat that includes their many storied years in Brooklyn). Don also leads all Dodger pitchers in games played, games started, shutouts, innings pitched, and strikeouts.

★   ★   ★   ★   ★

Although best known as a Dodger, Don was also a member of both the 1982 pennant-winning Milwaukee Brewers (a great club!) and the 1986 division-winning California Angels.

★   ★   ★   ★   ★

No player in the modern era has gone as many at-bats without a single home run as Don Sutton.

★   ★   ★   ★   ★

Although "Black and Decker" pitched 5 1-hitters and 9 2-hitters, the elusive no-hitter never happened for him. How's that for tough luck?

Follies Factoids

Mickey Mantle, over the course of his eighteen-year career, only faced nine different teams during the regular season. Derek Jeter, by contrast, has squared off against twenty-nine different ball clubs.

Since 1871, Boston has been the only city that has hosted a professional baseball team each and every year.

Much has been made of how the Chicago Cubs have gone a century without a baseball championship. However, San Francisco, Houston, San Diego, Dallas/Fort Worth, Seattle, Denver, and Tampa/St. Pete have all yet to win their **FIRST** world championship.

There has never been a New York Yankee championship team of the twenty-six that did not have at least one of the four following men in pinstripes as either a player or coach: Lou Gehrig, Bill Dickey, Yogi Berra, Willie Randolph.

There have been truly great players who never managed to play in an All-Star Game. Ty Cobb and Kirk Gibson are among them. Of course, there was no All-Star Game during Cobb's playing career.

Who is the best current player who has yet to make it into an All-Star Game? It's debatable, but the conversation would have to include the following players, all of whom have strung together impressive careers: Pat Burrell, Eric Chavez, Travis Hafner, Juan Pierre (my choice), Shannon Stewart, Mike Timlin, Tim Wakefield, and Chien Ming-Wang.

42

TWENTY-ONE PITCHERS WHO COULD WIELD A BAT

1. In 1903, the Pirates' *Brickyard Kennedy* hit .362 and slugged .534.

2. In 1913, *Earl "Chink" Yingling* of the Brooklyn Superbas hit .383 in 60 at-bats.

3. In 1923, the Giants' *Jack Bentley* hit .427, slugged .573, and knocked in fourteen runners.

4. In 1925, thirty-seven-year-old *Walter "Big Train" Johnson* of the Senators hit .433 with 20 RBIs. The Pride of Kansas would end his career with an impressive 547 hits and 255 RBIs.

5. In 1930, *Red Ruffing* compiled a .364 batting average, one of seven seasons in which he hit at least .300. The hurler would end up with 521 hits and 36 homers.

6. In 1935, *Wes Ferrell* of the Red Sox hit .347 with 7 homers. Ferrell retired in 1941 with 38 career home runs.

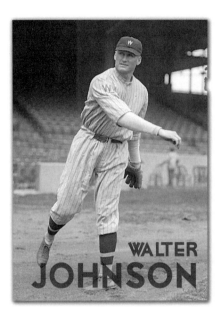

7.   In 1937, *Jim "Abba Dabba" Tobin* hit .441 for the Pirates. Later in his career, he enjoyed a game in which he not only hit 3 homers but also made an additional out on the warning track.

8.   In 1947, prior to his managerial days, Detroit's *Fred Hutchinson* hit .302 with 33 hits.

9.   In 1949, *Bob Lemon* slugged .556 for the Cleveland Indians. Lemon retired with 37 homers, 148 runs, and 147 RBIs.

10. In 1951, *Carl Scheib* of the Philadelphia Athletics hit .396 with 2 doubles, 2 triples, and 2 homers.

11. In 1955, the Dodgers' *Don Newcombe* hit .355 with 7 homers.

12. In 1958, *Warren Spahn* on the Milwaukee Braves hit .333 (36 for 108). Spahn retired with 35 homers and 189 RBIs.

13.   In 1965, the Dodgers' *Don Drysdale* hit .300 with 7 homers.

14.   In 1970, *Bob Gibson* of the Cardinals hit .303 with 19 RBIs.

15.   In 1971, *Catfish Hunter* hit .350 (36 for 103) and knocked in 12 runs for the Oakland A's.

16.   In 1980, *Don Robinson* hit .333 in 57 at-bats for the Pirates. "Caveman" would clear the .300 barrier in three seasons, but his best year as a slugger was probably 1982, when he hit .282 with 2 homers and 16 RBIs.

17.   In 1993, *Orel Hershiser* hit .356 (26 for 73) and scored 11 runs to help the Dodger cause.

18.   In 2002, *Mike Hampton* of the Rockies hit .344 with 3 homers. The previous season, he parked 7 homers.

19.   In 2003, *Brooks Kieschnick* of the Brewers redefined the role of utility player when he not only pitched in forty-two games, but also played an additional twenty-seven games as a left fielder, designated hitter, or pinch hitter. Overall, he hit .300 with 7 homers.

20.   In 2007, *Micah Owings* of the Diamondbacks went 20 for 60 with 4 home runs and a .683 slugging permillage. His productivity was such that the hurler even was utilized as a pinch hitter six times.

21.   In 2008, *Carlos Zambrano* not only won fourteen games for the Cubs, he hit .337, slugged .554, and cranked out 4 homers.

43

INTERLEAGUE PLAY

◇◇

CHICAGO CUBS

In the first twelve seasons since interleague play began in 1997, the Cubbies competed in 172 contests against American League teams (an average of over fourteen games per year).

Some seasons, they played as many as eighteen games while in other years, they played as few as twelve.

Whether they were at home or on the road, here are the number of times the Cubs played against their junior league counterparts during this initial twelve-year span:

Chicago White Sox (66)   Seattle Mariners (6)
Minnesota Twins (18)   Texas Rangers (6)
Kansas City Royals (15)   Tampa Bay Rays (6)
Cleveland Indians (11)   Boston Red Sox (3)
Detroit Tigers (11)   X   Milwaukee Brewers (3)
Toronto Blue Jays (9)   - *the 1997 AL version*
Baltimore Orioles (6)   Oakland Athletics (3)
New York Yankees (6)   Los Angeles Angels of Anaheim (0)

Although they've often played in the Arizona preseason, the Angels and Cubs have never played a single meaningful contest—at least through 2008.

In addition, during this initial span, the Red Sox have never once visited Wrigley Field—although the Bosox did pass through the friendly confines en route to winning the 1918 World Series.

MILWAUKEE BREWERS

One year after interleague play began in 1997, the Milwaukee Brewers switched leagues, giving them the lone distinction of having played interleague games against both National and American League clubs. Within the initial dozen-year interim, they played 169 contests (an average of just over fourteen games per season).

Whether they were home or away, here are the number of times the Brew Crew played against their cross-league counterparts during the first twelve seasons of cross-league ball.

Minnesota Twins (52)	Cincinnati Reds (3)
Detroit Tigers (18)	Houston Astros (3)
Kansas City Royals (18)	Oakland Athletics (3)
Cleveland Indians (15)	New York Yankees (3)
Chicago White Sox (12)	Pittsburgh Pirates (3)
Baltimore Orioles (6)	Seattle Mariners (3)
Boston Red Sox (6)	St. Louis Cardinals (3)
Los Angeles Angels (6)	Texas Rangers (3)
Toronto Blue Jays (6)	Tampa Bay Devil Rays (3)
Chicago Cubs (3)	

As of press time, Tampa Bay has yet to play in Milwaukee, whereas both the A's and Rangers haven't had the pleasure of visiting Wisconsin since 1996.

NEW YORK YANKEES

In the first dozen years since the inception of interleague play, the Yankees participated in 210 contests against National League teams (an average of 17.5 games per year).

Whether they were at home or on the road, here are the number of times the Yanks played against each of those NL teams during that time frame:

New York Mets (66)   Chicago Cubs (6)

Atlanta Braves (19)

Philadelphia Phillies (18)

Florida Marlins (17)

Montreal Expos (15)

Arizona Diamondbacks (9)

Colorado Rockies (9)

Pittsburgh Pirates (9)

San Diego Padres (9)

Cincinnati Reds (6)

San Francisco Giants (6)

St. Louis Cardinals (6)

Houston Astros (6)

Los Angeles Dodgers (3)

Milwaukee Brewers (3)

- the NL version

Washington Nationals (3)

Although the Bombers played against every single National League franchise from 1997–2008, they never managed to host the Washington Nationals, the NL version of the Milwaukee Brewers, or the Los Angeles Dodgers. However, Dodger Blue has plenty of experience in the House that Ruth Built, having played World Series games there in 1977, 1978, and 1981.

Follies Factoids

The initial year that interleague play took place, overall attendance increased by 3,071,308 (a surge of 5.1% over the previous year's total).

In the first twelve years of interleague play: American League clubs were victorious nearly 52% of the time; the Montreal Expos/Washington Nationals franchise played forty-seven more interleague games than did the Pittsburgh Pirates; and of all thirty teams, the New York Yankees racked up the best winning permillage (.586).

44

THE SWITCH IS ON

◇◇

June 19, 2008

At a minor league game in Brooklyn, the contest had to be delayed in the ninth inning for an incredibly unusual reason.

Nah, it wasn't raining and, no, it wasn't because the players had spilled out of the dugouts to brawl. Neither scenario would be all that unusual.

This particular game was interrupted because both the hitter and pitcher began behaving like schizophrenics. Here's what happened:

The Class A Staten Island Yankees were visiting Coney Island to play the Cyclones in a New York-Penn League game. After eight innings, the Yanks had built up a comfortable 7–2 lead. To nail down the ninth inning, they sent Pat Venditte to the mound. The right-hander quickly retired the first two hitters, but the third batter nailed a single to keep the Cyclones' hopes swirling.

At this point, switch hitter Nicholas Giarraputo strolled into the batter's box. Of course, against the righty, he prepared to hit left-handed. However, Pat Venditte was no ordinary pitcher—because he, too, was ambidextrous.

Pat simply moved his double-thumbed hybrid glove to the other hand, shifted, and prepared to throw southpaw. Such a move would also help him keep the runner at first base more honest.

But before Pat could wind-up, Nicholas deftly traipsed the plate and swiveled so that he could hit left-handed. Tit for tat.

In response, the hurler switched the glove back to his left hand and placed his right foot on the rubber. Tat for tit. All the while, people in the stands began rubbing their eyes as though they were hallucinating.

Quickly, the hitter moved across the plate again, prompting yet another glove switch, which caused Nicholas to jump back to the far side of the plate yet again.

Apparently, a hoe down had broken out in Brooklyn.

Despite the tension, laughter began to pour out of both dugouts. Many of the fans were enjoying the unprecedented scene as well. But that laughter had not made its way to the playing field.

Pat left the pitching mound and began to intensely jaw with the umpires. There was no end in sight to the stalemate, so the umpires concluded that Nicholas would have to commit to a single side of the plate.

Over three minutes had elapsed since Venditte had thrown a pitch, but play could finally resume.

Four pitches later, the game ended. Nicholas, hitting from the right side, swung and missed at a ball thrown from the north paw of Pat. So it went, that within this particular matchup, both players managed to be right.

Follies Puzzle Clue

QUESTION: If you were at Turner Field in Atlanta and you had to go to the nearest major league stadium, what city would you depart for?

CLUE: If you said either Washington DC, or St. Louis, you would be wrong.

(An additional clue appears on page 194.)

45

THE CHANGING ROLE OF THE CLOSER (1950-2005)

◇◇

1950   *Jim Konstanty* of the pennant-winning Phillies led all of baseball with 22 saves (his average stint: 2.05 innings).

1955   *Ray Narleski* of the second-place Indians led everyone with 19 saves (his average stint: 1.86 innings).

1960   *Lindy McDaniel* of the third-place Cardinals led with 26 saves (his average stint: 1.78 innings).

1965   *Ted Abernathy* of the eighth-place Cubs led with 31 saves (his average stint: 1.62 innings).

1970   *Wayne Granger* of the pennant-winning Reds led with 35 saves (his average stint: 1.26 innings).

1975   *Goose Gossage* of the fifth-place White Sox led with 26 saves (his average stint: 2.29 innings).

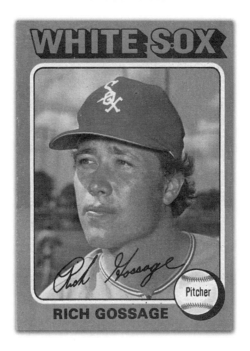

WHITE SOX

Pitcher

RICH GOSSAGE

1980   *Goose Gossage* of the Eastern Division-winning Yankees and *Dan Quisenberry* of the pennant-winning Royals tied for the major league lead with 33 saves (their average stints: 1.55 and 1.71 innings respectively).

1985   *Jeff Reardon* of the third-place Expos led with 41 saves (his average stint: 1.39 innings).

1990   *Bobby Thigpen* of the second-place White Sox led with 57 saves (his average stint: 1.15 innings).

1995   *Jose Mesa* of the pennant-winning Indians led with 46 saves   ✗ (his average stint: 1.03 innings).

2000   *Antonio Alfonseca* of the third-place Marlins led with 45 saves (his average stint: 1.03 innings).

2005   *Chad Cordero* of the last-place Nationals led with 47 saves (his average stint: 1.00 innings).

As the role of the fireman evolved to where he was almost solely used as a force in the ninth inning, the importance of the middle relief corps has increased accordingly. In looking at Jose Mesa's success with the Cleveland Indians in 1995, it's clear that he would have never been handed so many games to save had it not been for the exemplary work of unsung middle relievers Paul Assenmacher, Eric Plunk, and Julian Taveras. The trio pitched 187.3 innings and combined to go 22–6 with a 2.59 ERA.

Follies Factoids

The only player ever to lead baseball in saves for three consecutive years is Firpo Marberry, who pulled off the hat trick from 1924 to 1926.

Firpo Marberry was also the first reliever in history to reach the 100-save total.

A precursor to the "scary" relievers of more recent years, Marberry constantly wore a scowl on the mound. His intimidating glare reminded players and fans of heavyweight boxer Luis Firpo, which earned "Frederick" the nickname—a name he detested, causing him to scowl even more.

Follies Puzzle Clue

QUESTION: If you were at Turner Field in Atlanta and you had to go to the nearest major league stadium, what city would you depart for?
CLUE: If you said either St. Petersburg or Tampa, you would still be wrong (The answer to the question appears on page 199).

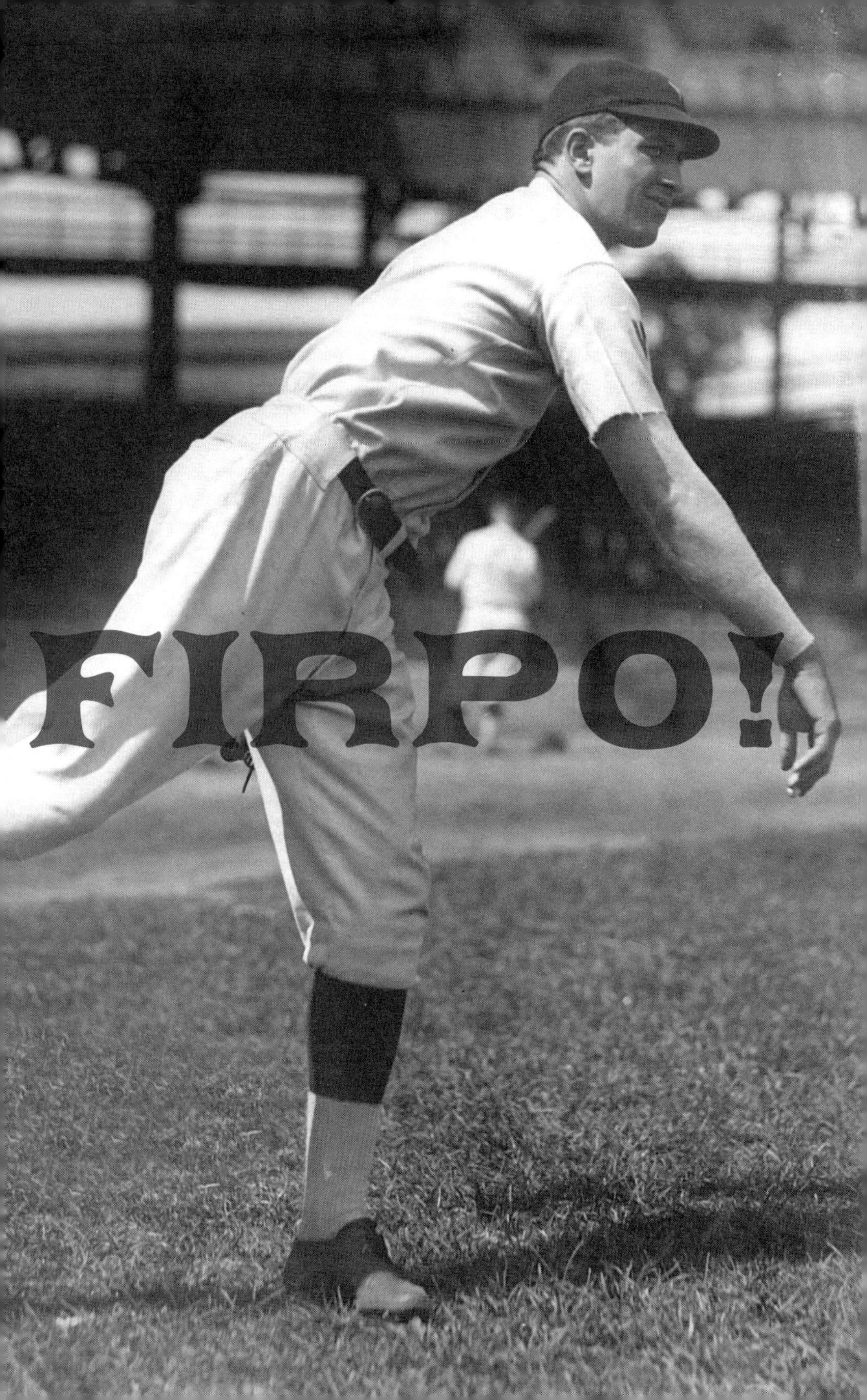
FIRPO!

46

THE ECCENTRIC ERIC BYRNES

efore he was three years old, Eric Byrnes managed to scale
a tree so high that the local fire department had to be called
into action. Although the incident put a damper on the
Byrnes family picnic, it did give fair warning of the thrill-seeking life-
style that was to follow.

The youngster was soon attracted to horizontal sports. However,
few were custom designed for an athlete of his unique disciplines.

Although he was talented enough to enter karate tournaments,
he often ended up getting disqualified for smacking his opponents
around with, shall we say, his more Western techniques. Tennis was
a similarly bad fit, as his racket was often used as a projectile—which
can be frowned upon by the more discriminating line judges.

But then there was baseball, which was the chocolate to Eric's
peanut butter. Although an excellent hitter, it was his kamikaze style
of defense that made him a player impossible not to admire. Somehow, the outfield fences he collided with ended up in worse shape
than he did. That takes talent.

On the field, Eric became a mixed bag of athletic talent, fierce
competitiveness, and all-out play...but sometimes, this mentality extended above and beyond the call of duty.

On one occasion in Oakland, a fan came out of the stands and

began running through the outfield. Most players would just take it easy until security tracked down the intruder, but not Eric. Suddenly morphing into a linebacker, he hit a fierce sprint and tackled the guy out of his shoes. The commissioner's office wasn't exactly thrilled with his impromptu Raider audition. His manager wasn't either. However, the Oakland Police Department was. They gifted Byrnsie with a baton and handcuffs in honor of his service.

But despite the intense play, Eric is also known as someone who can transform the personality of a clubhouse into a funhouse.

Baseball is a business, but Eric serves as a reminder to even the most jaded people that it can also be an opportunity for fun, even though his style of fun can sometimes lead to tremendous discomfort.

Many ballplayers have been known through the years to play crude practical jokes with Icy Hot (a medicinal cream that slowly heats up sore muscles), Byrnsie and friends took this prank to a whole new level.

They not only coated a teammate's jockstrap with it, but they also applied a thin layer to both his civilian underwear and to his entire suit. The genius of the plan was that they managed to do this after the game when the team had to quickly fly off to play in another city.

As such, the victim had the worst flight of his entire life and he sweated like a sausage on a barbecue. Being far from a shower and a fresh set of clothes, Eric's victim could do next to nothing about it—even with the advantage of having a tiny airplane lavatory at his disposal.

But having Eric around is good for winning baseball games, as his teams made it to the playoffs in four of his first eight seasons. Although his combination of speed, power, and defense are prime reasons, one can't help but wonder if the intangibles he brings to the clubhouse don't add fuel to these winning fires.

We asked his Arizona Diamondback teammate Conor Jackson about Eric's most unusual behaviors. A thoughtful expression came over Conor's face, as if he were having trouble paring the list down to a number lower than five hundred.

Cojak recalled a time when his friend struck out looking, but instead of retreating to the dugout, Eric headed to first base as if he had earned a walk. With every step down that line, people got more confused. Some even double-checked the scoreboard. But about halfway there, Eric stopped and blithely returned to the Diamondback dugout, subtly checking out everyone's confused expressions in the process and having a laugh.

Perhaps such behavior should be expected from a man who drives around in a van called the "Shaggin' Wagon," who has an affinity for surfing, and whose best-known nickname is "Crash Test Dummy." But a man of Eric's playful spirit is also ripe to have impractical jokes played on him.

On one occasion, his teammates snuck into his locker and tucked a salmon inside his mitt, leaving it there to work its odorizing magic. The prank was especially funny because Eric was known for having the crappiest mitt on the entire team, a tattered, fish-shaped piece of leather (nicknamed "the salmon") that looked like it had fallen out of a time machine from 1920.

When Eric opened his locker, he didn't notice anything amiss and to be fair, it's not like the errant fish smell didn't have competition. Eric just put on his uniform, tucked the mitt, and went out onto the field to stretch and take some swings.

All during the pregame activities, his teammates kept peaking over to see when he would catch on, but the prank just wasn't clicking. Finally, after an hour, Byrnsie opened his mitt to slip it on and his hand squished the fish.

His disgust reverberated throughout the stadium, and his cursing streak sent his teammates into gales of laughter for nearly thirty minutes. Of course, he didn't throw out the mitt. After all, that would be wasteful.

But Eric is a thinking man's eccentric and has been known to entertain people with his smarts as well. Once while driving with a teammate to a game, he found a placemat from a fast food restaurant that listed all of the US presidents in proper order. Eric's teammate bet him that he couldn't memorize the entire list within thirty minutes.

Eric not only took the bet, he won it. To this day, Eric can rattle off the presidential list like it's the alphabet, which probably makes him the only baseball player in history with a fish-scented mitt, a wagon built for shaggin', a credited football tackle, and the knowledge that Rutherford B. Hayes came before James A. Garfield.

Follies Puzzle Answer

QUESTION: If you were at Turner Field in Atlanta and you had to go to the nearest major league stadium, what city would you depart for?

ANSWER: If you answered Cincinnati, you would be correct. Great American Ballpark is a mere 450.8 miles from Turner Field, whereas Tropicana Field in St. Petersburg is 467.8 miles away.

47

THE COOPERSTOWN WALLFLOWERS

-WE NOW PRESENT-

A list of the great players who have come the CLOSEST,
year by year, to gaining election to the Hall of Fame.

However, this list is progressive because we have also gone
back and omitted the players who eventually gained entry.

Note: *There were no Hall of Fame elections in 1940, 1941
1943, 1944, 1957, 1959, 1961, 1963, or 1965.*

⇥ The Almost Hall-Of-Famers ⇤

Hal Chase *(1936)*
Johnny Kling *(1937-1939, 1942, 1945-1946)*
Nap Rucker *(1942)*
Smoky Joe Wood *(1947)*
Jimmie Wilson *(1948)*
Pepper Martin *(1949, 1958)*
Charlie Grimm *(1950)*

Hank Gowdy *(1951-1957)*
Lefty O'Doul *(1960)*
Marty Marion *(1962, 1969)*
Al Lopez *(1964, 1966-1967)*
Allie Reynolds *(1968)*
Gil Hodges *(1970-1983)*
Tony Oliva *(1984-1985, 1988-1992)*
Roger Maris *(1986-1987)*
Steve Garvey *(1993-1996, 1999-2001)*
Ron Santo *(1997-1998)*
Andre Dawson *(2002-2009)*

ACCUMULATIVE HALL OF FAME VOTES 2000-2009
(minimum 50 votes)

*Asterisk denotes a Hall-of-Famer

NAME	VOTES	BALLOTS	
Jim Rice*	3,144	10	
Goose Gossage*	2,487	9	
André Dawson	2,330	8	
Bert Blyleven	2,078	10	
Bruce Sutter*	1,986	7	
Jack Morris	1,613	10	X
Lee Smith	1,521	7	
Gary Carter*	1,312	4	
Tommy John	1,366	10	
Steve Garvey	1,087	8	
Ryne Sandberg*	946	3	
Dave Parker	724	10	
Don Mattingly	701	9	
Dale Murphy	677	10	
Dave Concepcion	591	9	
Alan Trammell	659	8	X
Cal Ripken Jr.*	537	1	
Tony Gwynn*	532	1	

ALMOST HALL-OF-FAMER

SMOKY JOE
WOOD

ACCUMULATIVE HALL OF FAME VOTES 2000-2009 (cont.)

Asterisk denotes a Hall-of-Famer

NAME	VOTES	BALLOTS
Rickey Henderson*	511	1
Jim Kaat	499	4
Wade Boggs*	474	1
Dave Winfield*	435	1
Ozzie Smith*	433	1
Paul Molitor*	431	1
Eddie Murray*	423	1
Kirby Puckett *	423	1
Dennis Eckersley *	421	1
Carlton Fisk*	397	1
Tony Perez*	385	1
Mark McGwire	374	3
Tim Raines	254	2
Luis Tiant	234	3
Keith Hernandez	174	5
Ron Guidry	94	3
Harold Baines	84	3
Orel Hershiser	82	2
Dave Stewart	61	2
Albert Belle	59	2
Fernando Valenzuela	50	2

48

FOUR-PEAT, FIVE-PEAT, THREE-PEAT

◇◇

Nowadays, the word "dynasty" gets thrown around a lot. It seems like every time a team manages to string together a few consecutive playoff appearances, the "D" word is invoked.

Of course, it's debatable as to what the definition of "dynasty" should be. I believe the minimum requirement should be that the team in question wins at least three consecutive world championships. After all, it's not like the Ming dynasty only managed to keep the Manchurians on the wrong side of the Great Wall of China every other year, right? Too arcane?

The Philadelphia Athletics from 1910-1913 were as dominant as were the 1915-1918 Boston Red Sox, but both teams had an off-year within their hot periods...so to me, neither can be considered a true dynasty.

In fact, only two baseball franchises in history have met my specific criterion. The first team to do so was the New York Yankees...and they actually managed this hat trick on three separate occasions.

The first time the Bronx Bombers pulled off a three-peat occurred during the throes of the Great Depression. In actuality, these Yankees from 1936–1939 managed to win four consecutive world championships. Nice!

Manager Joe McCarthy's rosters during this whiz-bang included such greats as Lou Gehrig, Bill Dickey, Lefty Gomez, Red Ruffing, and even a young Joe DiMaggio. Fittingly, these five players would all end up joining their skipper in the Hall of Fame.

The next Yankee dynasty lasted even longer (five consecutive seasons) and was triggered by the arrival of manager Casey Stengel in 1949. The Yankee Clipper (DiMaggio) was still around and contributed to this era as well.

Stengal's other key players during this unparalleled run included Yogi Berra, Whitey Ford, Johnny Mize, Phil Rizzuto, and a young Mickey Mantle. Fittingly, these five players would all end up joining their skipper in the Hall of Fame.

The last Yankee dynasty to date (1998-2000) occurred during Joe Torre's tenure as skipper. Torre's key players during this glory run included Bernie Williams, Mariano Rivera, Andy Pettitte, Derek Jeter, David Cone, and Roger Clemens. It's practically a foregone conclusion that Torre and at least a couple of these athletes will have plaques in Cooperstown and/or in Monument Park some day.

Clearly, the New York Yankees know the definition of the word "dynasty" as well as anyone, but I'm more than happy to say that you don't necessarily have to have been a Yankee to know the joy of having won three World Series championships in a row.

49

THE OAKLAND A'S DYNASTY (1972-1974)

◇◇◇

A TIMELINE OF HOW THE DYNASTY CAME TOGETHER

1960 *Charley Finley*, a Kansas City insurance mogul, after failing to outbid Gene Autry for the expansion Angels, instead buys the Kansas City Athletics in an estate sale.

1963 On September 9, infielder *Dick Green*, 22, is called up to the major league team. Green would prove to be the first piece of the championship puzzle.

1964 Shortstop *Bert Campaneris*, 22, catcher *Dave Duncan*, 18, and pitcher *Johnny Odom*, 19, all debut.

1965 A nineteen-year-old named *Jim Hunter* makes it to the show. Finley would later nickname him "*Catfish*."

1966 Third baseman (and future captain) *Sal Bando*, 22, joins the squad. Catfish Hunter makes his initial appearance as an all-star.

1967 Outfielders *Joe Rudi*, 20, and *Reggie Jackson*, 21, both come aboard. Reserve infielder *Ted Kubiak*, 25, joins as well.

1968 *Charley Finley moves the franchise* from Kansas City, Missouri, to Oakland, California. *Sal Bando, Dave Duncan, Reggie Jackson*, and *Joe Rudi* all become regulars in the starting lineup. "*Campy*" *Campaneris* and "*Blue Moon*" *Odom* are both selected to the all-star team. Late in the season, a clean-shaven twenty-two-year-old starting pitcher (*yours truly*) is added to the mix. When all is said and done, this Oakland team posts a winning record—the franchise's first since 1952.

1969   Twenty-two-year old catcher *Gene Tenace* joins up, as does a nineteen-year-old fireballer named *Vida Blue*. Sal Bando and Reggie Jackson both become all-stars for the first time. The ball club improves by six games and ends up in second place in the newly formed American League West.

1970   *Charley Finley shortens the team's nickname* to the A's. For the second consecutive year, we post a winning record, but finish nine games behind Harmon Killebrew, Tony Oliva, Rod Carew, and the rest of the tough Minnesota Twins.

1971   *Dick Williams* becomes our manager. On May 8, first baseman *Mike Epstein* and key reliever *Darold Knowles* arrive in a trade. On May 16, Williams pulls me out of the rotation and makes me his closer. Catcher *Dave Duncan* becomes an all-star. *Vida Blue* goes all-universe and not only wins the Cy Young Award with his twenty-four victories but is awarded the league MVP too.

THE EMERGENCE

Our team won the American League West in 1971. It was the first time the Athletics franchise had made it to the postseason since 1931. You might say that the champagne flowed a little bit.

However, our party was short-lived. Boog Powell and the mighty Baltimore Orioles swept us in the divisional playoffs. Life is unfair.

But in the aftermath of this squish, the nucleus of our talented young club stayed intact—and got a year older, a year wiser, and a year better. In addition, our pitching rotation got bolstered from an offseason trade that brought aboard starter Ken Holtzman.

Over the next three seasons, Holtzman, Catfish Hunter, Vida Blue, and Blue Moon Odom would form a formidable quartet. In baseball, as it is in poker, it's nearly impossible to beat four aces.

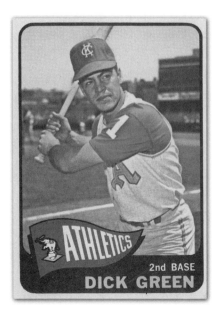

ATHLETICS

2nd BASE
DICK GREEN

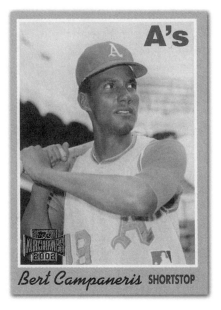

A's

Bert Campaneris SHORTSTOP

THE OAKLAND LOOK

Although our roster hadn't undergone a massive transformation prior to our first championship, we did undergo a cosmetic one. In 1972, we all began to wear those famous bold green and solid gold jerseys. These might not seem gaudy by today's standards, but at the time, every other team was wearing standard home whites and road gray. To the staunch traditionalists, we looked like beer leaguers who had wandered onto the wrong baseball diamond.

But there was yet another cosmetic shift we underwent that similarly became a part of baseball folklore—and it would have never happened if not for legendary slugger Reggie Jackson.

During preseason, Reg had taken it upon himself to grow a scraggly beard. To say that his attempt at facial hair was unsightly would be like saying the *Titanic* had a small leak. Jackson's "beard" basically looked like a spotty comb-over that had somehow slipped all the way down to intermittent points on his jawbone.

To avoid traumatizing innocent women and children, my teammates and I decided that, for humanitarian purposes, we needed to hatch a plan to force him to shave.

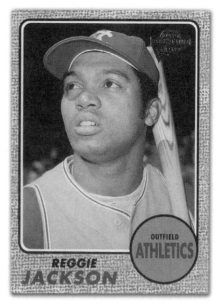

Our plan?

We all grew gnarly facial hair . Our hope was that management would have no choice but to ban all facial hair, including Reggie's.

But our diabolical plan backfired!!

When owner Charley Finley saw what we had done, he had one of his grand visions. He offered a $300 bonus to any player who could sport a moustache in time for the first game of the season. That was actually a week's pay for some of us. So it came to pass that on Opening Day, Finley's wallet got $7500 lighter.

As for me, I thought I'd make my moustache a little different from the rest, so I grew it way out and started using wax on the ends. Even with the name *Fingers,* I began to stick out like a sore thumb.

Our team opened the season by going 12–4, an impressive clip. Now, if we had opened up 4–12, I'm fairly certain that most of us would have shaved, but not wanting to upset the apple cart, the Moustache Gang remained intact.

Sure, we may have looked like a motley crew of mountain men, hippies, bikers, nineteenth-century gunslingers, and barbershop quartet members (all dressed up like colorblind little leaguers), but we had great fun— and as you are probably aware, we sure could play the game of baseball.

OUR SIX POSTSEASON OPPONENTS (1972-1974)
Billy Martin's *Detroit Tigers*
Earl Weaver's *Baltimore Orioles* (twice)
Sparky Anderson's *Cincinnati Reds*
Yogi Berra's *New York Mets*
Walter Alston's *Los Angeles Dodgers*

THE HALL OF FAMERS WE BATTLED DURING THESE THREE POSTSEASONS

Al Kaline	Brooks Robinson
Johnny Bench	Willie Mays
Joe Morgan	Tom Seaver
Tony Perez	Don Sutton
Jim Palmer	

THE NEAR-SPOILERS
★ Joe Coleman *(Tigers)*: threw a 14-K shutout at us
★ Bobby Tolan *(Reds)*: had 6 RBIs and 5 steals against us
★ Jack Billingham *(Reds)*: held us scoreless for 13.2 innings.
★ Rusty Staub *(Mets)*: hit .423 at our expense with 6 RBIs

THREE IN A ROW
In those early days of '72, we didn't know that we were on the verge of a stretch in which we would win three straight divisional titles (by an average margin of five-and-a-half games). We also weren't aware that we would have the chance to avenge our playoff loss against the Orioles, and we definitely couldn't have predicted that we would win the next three world championships.

All told, seventy-five players contributed to the A's dynasty. It would be difficult to select the best twenty-five-man Oakland team from this large pool, so we've instead put one together based solely on prolificacy.

The following team is made up of the nine pitchers who hurled the most innings along with the sixteen hitters who had the most at-bats during our three-year run at the top.

THE TWENTY-FIVE-MAN OAKLAND A'S DYNASTY TEAM

(Combined statistics from 1972–1974 including our thirty-three postseason games)

PITCHING STAFF

	Won-Loss	ERA	Strikeouts	Saves
Jim "Catfish" Hunter	74-25	2.56	501	
Ken Holtzman	65-43	2.79	440	
Vida Blue	44-38	3.21	480	
John "Blue Moon" Odom	24-24	3.25	248	
Dave Hamilton	20-14	3.48	159	
Glenn Abbott	6-7	3.11	44	
Darold Knowles	14-12	2.77	105	25
Paul Lindblad	6-9	2.68	80	8
Rollie Fingers	30-25	2.24	352	69

POSITION PLAYERS

Position		AVG	HR	RBI	SB
C	Ray Fosse	.234	13	82	
1B	Gene Tenace	.230	59	203	
2B	Dick Green	.232	5	70	
SS	Bert Campaneris	.259	17	130	126
3B	Sal Bando	.253	70	287	
LF	Joe Rudi	.290	56	255	
CF	Billy North	.266	9	67	108
RF	Reggie Jackson	.280	88	295	59
DH	Deron Johnson	.231	26	104	

RESERVES

Position		AVG	HR	RBI
C	Dave Duncan	.217	19	59
1B	Mike Epstein	.259	27	71
2B	Ted Kubiak	.209	3	44
RF	Angel Mangual	.232	6	32
RF	Matty Alou	.265	1	18
DH	Jesus Alou	.276	3	30
DH	Claudell Washington	.293	0	19

Follies Factoids

Three players on the 1971 Oakland team who just missed the parade were Mudcat Grant, infielder Tony La Russa, and future all-star outfielder Rick Monday.

Rick Monday was the player traded for Ken Holtzman. Earlier that off-season, there were separate discussions that would have sent Rick to the St. Louis Cardinals in exchange for Steve Carlton.

Don Sutton was almost part of the Athletic franchise as well, but Charley Finley didn't feel his name was catchy enough and took a pass on the future Hall of Famer. If only **Don Sutton** had been named after a color or a body part.

Conversely, as a prospect, I once considered signing with the Dodgers, but didn't want to get stuck in their pitching-rich minor league farm system.

Six members from the aforementioned twenty-five-man dynasty team, including myself, attended high school in California, by far the largest source of the A's talent pool.

The first of our three championships was won without Reggie Jackson, as he was felled by an unfortunate injury in the ALCS against the Detroit Tigers. Fortunately for us, we were a drink that did not require a straw to stir it.

Fleet center fielder Billy North was, ironically, the first designated hitter in Oakland A's history.

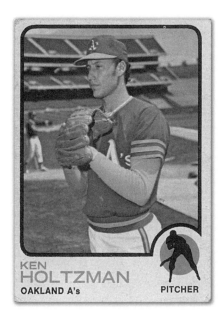

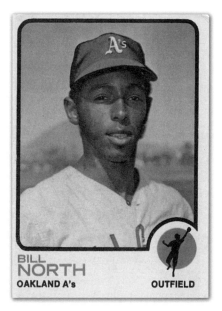

THE GREEN AND GOLD REVOLVING DOOR

Besides the twenty-five players already listed, other contributors to the A's dynasty included:

★ Pitchers: Joe Horlen, Bob Locker, Horatio Pina, and Diego Segui

★ Catchers: Larry Haney and Tim Hosley

★ Infielders: Pat Borque, Larry Brown, Tim Cullen, Mike Hegan, Dal Maxville, and Rich McKinney

★ Outfielders: Billy Conigliaro, Vic Davalillo, Jay Johnstone, and Bill Voss

★ Former all-stars: Rico Carty, Orlando Cepeda, and Denny McLain

★ Future all-stars: Phil Garner, George Hendrick, and Manny Trillo

RETOOLING AND REFUELING

1972 Veteran *Matty Alou* joins the club in midseason as do rookies *Dave Hamilton* and *Angel Mangual*.

1972 During the offseason, Charlie Finley trades our starting catcher (*Dave Duncan*), starting first baseman (*Mike Epstein*), and his fourth outfielder (*Matty Alou*). Players received in exchange include *Ray Fosse, Paul Lindblad,* and *Billy North.*

1973   *Reggie Jackson* is moved from centerfield to right. Additionally, catcher *Gene Tenace* shifts to first base. In midseason, backup outfielder *Jesus Alou* (Matty's brother) joins the team, as does designated hitter *Deron Johnson.* Pitcher *Glenn Abbott* is brought up from the minors, as is infielder *Phil Garner.*

1973   During the offseason, after managing the "Swinging A's" to their second consecutive championship, *Dick Williams* quits in a dispute with the owner. His successor is *Alvin Dark,* who previously managed the Athletics in 1966 and 1967.

1974   In midseason, Charlie Finley trades designated hitter *Deron Johnson.* Rookie outfielder *Claudell Washington* is brought up from the minors and instantly contributes to our third consecutive championship team.

Follies Tough Trivia Question

Name the five people enshrined in Cooperstown who were with for the A's during the 1972-1974 dynasty years (Answer on page 217).

INDIVIDUAL ACHIEVEMENTS DURING
THE DYNASTY RUN

1972   *Bert "Campy" Campaneris* leads the league both in steals (52) and in sacrifice hits (20). *Joe Rudi* tops the league in hits (181) and ties for the lead in triples (9). *Paul Lindblad* leads every pitcher in baseball in appearances (66). *Gene Tenace* is the World Series Most Valuable Player.

1973   *Reggie Jackson* wins the American League MVP Award. Jackson finishes first in home runs (32), runs scored (99), RBIs (117), and in slugging permillage (.531). *Sal Bando* ties for the league lead both in total bases (295) and for games played (162). *Reggie Jackson* also becomes the MVP of the World Series.

1974   *Catfish Hunter* wins the AL Cy Young Award. Catfish also wins the league ERA crown (2.49) and ties for the most victories in either league with twenty-five. *Joe Rudi* leads the league in total bases (287). *Reggie Jackson* leads the junior circuit in intentional walks (20). *Billy North* is the league's stolen base leader with 54. *Gene Tenace* leads the AL in bases on balls with 110. I, *Rollie Fingers*, wind up as the league leader in appearances with 76 and am also named the MVP of the World Series. Our captain, *Sal Bando*, leads all of baseball with 13 sacrifice flies.

THE DYNASTY'S ALL-STAR REPRESENTATIVES

★ 1972 ★	★ 1973 ★	★ 1974 ★
Sal Bando	Sal Bando	Sal Bando
Bert Campaneris	Bert Campaneris	Bert Campaneris
Catfish Hunter	Catfish Hunter	Catfish Hunter
Ken Holtzman	Rollie Fingers	Rollie Fingers
Reggie Jackson	Ken Holtzman	Reggie Jackson
Joe Rudi	Reggie Jackson	Joe Rudi

THE A'S AFTERMATH

1975 Even without *Catfish Hunter*, who departs through free agency, we win our fifth consecutive divisional title. However, the powerhouse Boston Red Sox prevent us from winning another pennant. After the loss, our skipper, *Alvin Dark*, is fired.

1976 Finley trades *Reggie Jackson* and *Ken Holtzman* prior to the start of the season. We finish in second place, two-and-a-half games behind the rising Kansas City Royals. After the season, *Bando, Campy, Rudi, Tenace,* and *I* all leave the team as free agents. In addition, *Phil Garner* and *Claudell Washington* are traded.

1977 The only players remaining on the team from the glory run are *Vida Blue* and *Billy North*. The team loses ninety-eight games and finishes in last place—beneath even the expansion Seattle Mariners. An A's rebirth of sorts takes place in the Bronx where *Catfish Hunter, Reggie Jackson,* and *Ken Holtzman* re-unite as teammates on the New York Yankees. "Oakland East" wins yet another world championship.

1978 In May, *Billy North*, the final link to the A's dynasty, is traded, effectively completing the dismantling. The Yankees win yet another world championship, but this time it is four former A's players who contribute, as *Paul Lindblad* joins the team in midseason.

1979   The Pittsburgh Pirates win the World Series, and former Oakland standout *Phil Garner* goes 12 for 24 in the Fall Classic to help them get there.

1980   The Philadelphia Phillies win the World Series, and former Oakland infielder *Manny Trillo* is their starting second baseman.

1980   *Charlie Finley* sells the team, ending his twenty-one-year tenure as owner and general manager of the Athletics franchise.

1981   The Los Angeles Dodgers win the World Series, and former Oakland outfielder *Jay Johnstone* hits .667 in the Fall Classic to help them get there.

1982   *Joe Rudi* returns to Oakland to play his final season in the major leagues. The St. Louis Cardinals win the World Series, and *George Hendrick* (Oakland's fifth outfielder in 1972) hits .321 in the Fall Classic to help them get there. The Cardinal's backup catcher is *Gene Tenace*—who adds another championship ring to his collection. The ball club they beat was my team at the time, the Milwaukee Brewers. Unfortunately, I had to miss the Series due to injury. But I wasn't the only Brewer with Oakland roots, as the recently retired *Sal Bando* was upstairs helping run things in the front office.

1987   Following in Joe Rudi's footsteps, *Reggie Jackson* returns to Oakland for one season to finish out his playing days.

1990   After a seventeen-year career, *Claudell Washington*, the final active player from the Oakland A's dynasty, retires.

1991   *Gene Tenace* briefly becomes the manager of the Toronto Blue Jays.

1992   *Phil Garner* begins a lengthy career as a big league manager.

2009   *Dave Duncan* enters his thirty-second year as a major league coach (and counting). Many consider him to be one of the best, if not the very best, pitching coach in major league history.

Follies Tough Trivia Answer

The five people enshrined in Cooperstown who were around for at least a portion of the Oakland A's dynasty years 1972-1974 are Orlando Cepeda, Catfish Hunter, Reggie Jackson, Dick Williams, and myself. (Cepeda appeared in three games for Oakland during the 1972 season.)

Follies Factoids

Twelve Oakland players went bell to bell from the beginning of 1972 to the final game of the 1974 World Series, not including Vida Blue who missed the beginning of '72 due to a contract dispute. The year prior, Vida posted a 24-8 record alongside a 1.82 ERA. In addition, stadium attendance spiked whenever he was scheduled to take the mound. Blue earned a salary of $14,750 in 1971. In 2009 dollars, that works out to about $80,000. How times have changed.

During the dynasty run, Deron Johnson and Paul Lindblad were both on their second tour of duty with the Athletics. Lindblad had actually been part of the package that brought Mike Epstein and Darold Knowles to the club.

Joe Rudi and Reggie Jackson weren't the only two players from the dynasty years to return to Oakland. Dave Hamilton and Tim Hosley did as well. In addition, Dave Duncan returned to the Oakland Coliseum as the A's pitching coach from 1985 to 1994.

50

THE FORGOTTEN THIRD BASEMAN

◇◇

From 1902 to 1910, fans on the North side of Chicago were amazed by their hometown infield. Shortstop Joe Tinker, second sacker Johnny Evers, and first baseman Frank Chance were so adept at turning double plays that a 1910 poem, titled "Baseball's Sad Lexicon" was written in their honor by a rueful fan of the New York Giants.

> *These are the saddest of possible words:*
> *"Tinker to Evers to Chance."*
> *Trio of bear cubs, and fleeter than birds,*
> *Tinker and Evers and Chance.*
> *Ruthlessly pricking our gonfalon bubble,*
> *Making a Giant hit into a double—*
> *Words that are heavy with nothing but trouble:*
> *"Tinker to Evers to Chance."*

Just as the poet Longfellow immortalized Paul Revere, Franklin Pierce Adams immortalized the acrobatic trio, as their names all remain famous to this day.

But who, except experts in baseball history, remembers the fourth member of this historic infield? If the truth be told: hardly anyone. And we aim to right that wrong.

Although Doc Casey managed to put in 388 games at third base during the Tinker to Evers to Chance era, the trio's primary partner was Harry Steinfeldt, an accomplished hitter who usually bested the famous trio when it came to slugging the old gonfalon bubble. In fact, Harry led the National League in hits and RBIs in 1906. He put in 730 games at the hot corner for those great Chicago teams, and we suspect he took part in his fair share of double plays as well.

Alas, if only his name had been as catchy as his glove.

Mr. Harry Steinfeldt sits in a car on a baseball field, circa 1906. The reason for this odd photo, like Harry himself, is lost in history.

51

AN EVOLUTIONARY TIMELINE OF BASEBALL SINCE 1901

(With special nods to Babe Ruth and Nolan Ryan)

1901   The *American League* debuts with eight teams.
        The *Chicago White Sox* and *Detroit Tigers* both begin
        play.
        Major League Baseball attracts *three million fans* for the
        first time.

1903   After a name change, the *Chicago Cubs* officially begin play.
        The *first World Series* (as we now know it) is played. The
        upstart Boston team (from the junior league) defeats the
        heavily favored Pittsburgh Pirates in a nine-game series.

1904   The New York Giants *boycott* the World Series claiming
        superiority over the entire American League.
        Major League Baseball attracts *four million fans* for the
        first time.
        The *pitching mound* is officially recognized.
        The game adopts a standard *154-game schedule*.

1905   The World Series is played again, but this time it is
        changed into a best of *seven-game* affair.
        Major League Baseball attracts *five million fans* for the
        first time.

1907   Major League Baseball attracts *six million fans* for the first time.

1908   After a name change, the *Boston Red Sox* officially begin play.
Shinguards are introduced.
The song *Take Me Out to the Ballgame* debuts.
The *Chicago Cubs* win their final world championship to date.
This season marks the lowest offensive output in history with teams posting an *average of only 3.38 runs per team per game.*
Major League Baseball attracts *seven million fans* for the first time.

1912   *Fenway Park* in Boston debuts.

1913   After a name change, the *New York Yankees* officially begin play.

1914   *Wrigley Field* in Chicago debuts.
Babe Ruth makes his major league debut.

1915   After a name change, the *Cleveland Indians* officially begin play.

1919   Once again, the World Series becomes a best-of-nine-games affair. Baseball is harmed by a *scandal* in which some players on the Chicago White Sox conspire to throw the World Series.

1920   *New bylaws* within the sport outlaw tampering with the baseball. The *dead ball era ends* and offensive output increases accordingly. Not so coincidentally, the career of slugger *Babe Ruth* begins to peak.
Baseball gloves begin to feature webs, forming a pocket between the thumb and index finger.
Major League Baseball breaks its 1908 attendance record by attracting in excess of *nine million fans.*
The most prominent of the *Negro Leagues* begins play.

1921   Baseball is first broadcast on the *radio.*

1922   The World Series reverts to a *best-of-seven* series.

1923   *Yankee Stadium* opens, dwarfing all the other ballparks.
The *Yankees* also win their first world championship.

1925   The minimum home run distance is set at *250 feet.*

1927   Babe Ruth becomes the first player to earn a *$70,000* annual salary.

1930   Baseball sets a new attendance record by attracting in excess of *ten million fans.*
        This proves to be the most offensive year in baseball history since 1897 with the *average output per game equaling 5.549 runs per team per game.*

1931   The Baseball Writers' *Most Valuable Player Awards* are given out for the first time.

1933   The first *All-Star Game* is played.

1935   The first *night game* in baseball history is played.
        Babe Ruth plays his last major league game.

1936   The *first five Hall of Famers* are selected (*Ty Cobb, Walter Johnson, Christy Mathewson, Babe Ruth, and Honus Wagner*).

1939   Baseball is *first broadcast on television.*
        The *Hall of Fame in Cooperstown* is officially dedicated.

1940   The first *Rookie of the Year Award* is given.

1941   *Joe DiMaggio* hits safely in fifty-six consecutive games.

1945   Baseball breaks the 1930 attendance record by attracting in excess of *10.8 million fans.*

1946   For the first time ever, the average baseball crowd holds in excess of *ten thousand fans.*

1947   *Jackie Robinson* becomes the first African-American player in years, breaking the color barrier.
        Nolan Ryan is born.

1948   *Babe Ruth* passes away.
        Attendance surpasses the *twenty million* mark for the first time.

1949   *Ted Williams* earns the first *$100,000* annual salary.
        Rookie of the Year Awards are given out in *both* leagues.

JOE DI MAGGIO
Salutes His Bat

1951   Baseball *telecasts* its first game in *color*.
Baseball also telecasts its first game from *coast to coast*.
The *Negro Leagues* has its last legitimate season.

1954   After a relocation, the newest version of the *Baltimore Orioles* begins play.
Players are no longer allowed to keep their gloves on the field between innings.

1956   The concept of *player/manager* falls out of vogue.
Ozzie Virgil, Sr. becomes the first player from the Dominican Republic to play in the major leagues.
Don Larsen pitches a perfect game in the World Series.
The *Cy Young Award* comes into existence.

1957   The *Dodgers* become the first baseball team to buy an *airplane*.

1958   After dual relocations, the *Los Angeles Dodgers* and *San Francisco Giants* both begin play.

1959   The minimum home run distance for new parks is set at *325 feet*.
Baseball begins playing *two* All-Star Games per year.

1960   The *names of players* begin to appear on the backs of uniforms.

1961   Major League Baseball *expands* from sixteen to eighteen teams.
The *Angels* franchise in Anaheim comes into existence.
After a relocation from Washington, the *Minnesota Twins* begin play.
The *nation's capital loses the Senator franchise* after sixty consecutive seasons, but is granted an expansion team that uses the "Senators" name.
Yankee *Roger Maris* sets the single-season record for home runs with 61.

1962   Baseball expands from eighteen teams to *twenty*.
Major League Baseball is introduced in *Houston*.
The *New York Mets* debut.
The game adapts a *162-game schedule*.

1962   *Dodger Stadium* opens for business. It will eventually become the third oldest stadium in baseball.

Baseball surpasses the attendance mark set in 1948.

1963   Baseball reverts to playing one All-Star Game per year.

1964   *Mr. Met* ushers in the mascot era.

1965   The *Astrodome*, baseball's first indoor facility, opens.

The *Colt 45s* change their name to *"Astros."*

1966   After a relocation from Milwaukee, the *Atlanta Braves* begin play.

For the first time in history, Major League Baseball surpasses *twenty-five million* in attendance.

Nolan Ryan makes his major league debut.

1967   For the first time, Cy Young Awards are given out in each league.

1968   After a relocation from Kansas City, the *Oakland Athletics* come into existence.

Pitching dominates, limiting opponents to a mere *3.41 runs per game.*

1969   Both leagues split into two divisions (East and West), thereby doubling the number of postseason berths from two to four.

Baseball expands from twenty to *twenty-four* teams.

The *Kansas City Royals* debut.

For the first time, baseball expands internationally with the formation of the *Montreal Expos.*

Major League Baseball debuts in *San Diego* when the Padres play their first game.

Seattle is introduced to Major League Baseball for the first time.

The *strike zone* is officially reduced and the *pitching mound* is lowered five inches, effectively giving hitters added advantages.

1970   After a relocation from Seattle, the newest version of the *Milwaukee Brewers* begins to play.

1971   All hitters are forced to wear protective *helmets.*

The *Washington Senators* cease to exist.

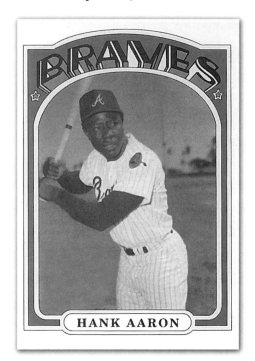

HANK AARON

1972   After a relocation from Washington, the *Texas Rangers* officially begin play.

The *Oakland Athletics* colorfully challenge the idea of what a uniform (and what a player) should look like.

Hank Aaron becomes the first player to earn a *$200,000* annual salary.

Curt Flood's challenge to the owner's reserve clause reaches the Supreme Court.

1973   The *designated hitter* is introduced.

Attendance cracks *thirty million* for the first time.

1974   *Hank Aaron* surpasses Babe Ruth's historic home run total.

1975   The *free agent era* begins, in large part due to Curt Flood's previous efforts.

Catfish Hunter becomes the first player to earn a *$740,000* annual salary.

1976   The Atlanta Braves begin broadcasting their games to other parts of the nation *via satellite*.

1977   Baseball expands to *twenty-six* teams with the dual debuts of the *Seattle Mariners* and the *Toronto Blue Jays*. For Toronto, it is their first taste of the major leagues. The *San Diego Chicken* triggers a wave of new mascots.

1978   Attendance tops *forty million* for the first time.

1979   *Nolan Ryan* becomes the first player to earn a *million-dollar annual salary*.
For the first time in history, the average baseball crowd holds in excess of *twenty thousand fans*.

1981   A *strike* hits baseball midseason. It is resolved, but the play-offs consist of twice as many teams (eight) when the first-half winners of each division play the second-half winners.

1983   *Nolan Ryan* becomes the all-time strikeout king for the first time, although he seesaws with Steve Carlton for the crown on numerous occasions.

1985   For the first time, the divisional playoffs are changed from being a five-game series to a *seven-game series*.

1987   Attendance cracks *fifty million* for the first time.

1989   A new state-of-the-art facility called the *Skydome* (now known as the Rogers Centre) debuts in Toronto.
Attendance cracks *fifty-five million* for the first time.

1991   *Roger Clemens* becomes the first player to earn a *five-million-dollar annual salary*.
Rickey Henderson becomes the game's all-time stolen base leader.

1992   *Oriole Park at Camden Yards* opens in Baltimore, a throwback stadium that greatly influences how future ballparks will be built.

1993   Baseball expands to *twenty-eight* teams with the addition of the *Colorado Rockies* and the *Florida Marlins*.
Nolan Ryan retires after twenty-seven seasons.
Baseball cracks *seventy million* in attendance, and for the first time the average crowd holds in excess of thirty-thousand people.

1994   Both the American and National Leagues realign to form *central* divisions.

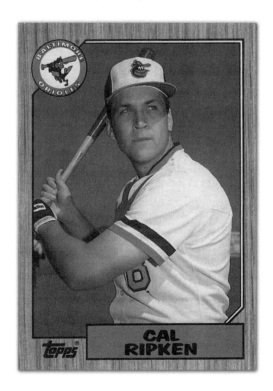

1994   A *strike* wipes out much of the season and the World Series.

1995   Japanese superstar *Hideo Nomo* is signed by the Los
       Angeles Dodgers, starting a wave that will bring thirty-
       five additional Japanese stars to America over the
       subsequent fourteen seasons.
       MLB.com, the official website of baseball, debuts.
       Cal Ripken Jr. breaks Lou Gehrig's consecutive game
       record.
       For the first time, *"wild card"* teams enter the postseason.

1996   *Albert Belle* becomes the first player to earn a ten-
       million-dollar annual salary.

1997   *Interleague play* is instituted. For the first time,
       geographic rivals such as the Mets/Yankees, Angels/
       Dodgers, and Astros/Rangers play meaningful games.

1998   Major League Baseball expands from twenty-eight to
       thirty teams.
       Baseball debuts in the *Tampa/St. Petersburg* area.

1998 Major League Baseball officially debuts in Phoenix as the *Arizona Diamondbacks* begin play.

The *Milwaukee Brewers* franchise, after twenty-eight seasons in the American League, *switches to the National League*.

Kevin Brown of the Dodgers becomes the first player to earn a *fifteen-million-dollar annual salary*.

Mark McGwire surpasses Roger Maris's single-season home run total, ending up with 70.

2000 *Alex Rodriguez* becomes the first player to earn a *twenty-five-million-dollar annual salary*.

Both the American and National Leagues set *all-time home run records*; numbers that have yet to be surpassed. All told, sixteen sluggers hit 40 home runs.

2001 *Barry Bonds* surpasses Mark McGwire's single season home run total, ending up with 73.

This season sees more strikeouts per game than in any preceding year in history. *Randy Johnson* leads with 372.

2002 Major League Baseball begins broadcasting games on the *internet*.

2005 After a relocation from Montreal, the newest version of the *Washington Nationals* begins play.

After a name change, the *Los Angeles Angels of Anaheim* officially begin play.

2006 Attendance cracks *seventy-five million* for the first time.

2007 *Barry Bonds* of the Giants becomes baseball's all-time home run champion, surpassing Henry Aaron's total of 755.

Craig Biggio, Barry Bonds, Roger Clemens, Julio Franco, Kenny Lofton, Mike Piazza, and Sammy Sosa all play their final game.

2008 After a name change, the *Tampa Bay Rays* begin play.

Nationals Park, the most expensive baseball facility built up to that time, opens in Washington D.C.

For the first time, the technology of *instant replay* is used by umpires.

2009 Both the *New York Mets* and *New York Yankees* introduce brand new state-of-the-art facilities.

52

NAME THAT CLOSER

◇◇

NAME THE FOLLOWING BASEBALL PERSONALITY
BASED ONLY ON THESE CLUES:

The Cleveland Indians once courted him.

He attended high school in California.

His co-workers included the likes of Tony La Russa and Joe Rudi.

He eventually became a member of the Bay Area Hall of Fame.

He often wore a distinctive moustache along with a hair style
that defied the image of "clean cut."

He was that rare relief pitcher who managed to win both
a Cy Young Award and a League Most Valuable Player Award.

Who is this Hall of Fame player?

(The answer can be found on page 234.)

53

THE HISTORICAL HOTBEDS OF BASEBALL

◇◇

In the decade of the 1890s, no single baseball venue drew as many fans as *League Park in Cincinnati*.

★ ★ ★ ★ ★

In the first decade of the 1900s, the *Polo Grounds in Manhattan* became the new hub of the national pastime.

★ ★ ★ ★ ★

In the 1910s, the epicenter of baseball's popularity migrated west to *Chicago's Comiskey Field*.

★ ★ ★ ★ ★

In the 1920s, the *Polo Grounds* once again became the mecca.

★ ★ ★ ★ ★

Yankee Stadium, just a cannon shot across the Harlem River from the Polo Grounds, drew more fans in the 1930s and 1940s than any other locale.

★ ★ ★ ★ ★

During the 1950s, the House That Ruth Built again reigned supreme. However, when Milwaukee got a major league team in 1953, *County Stadium* actually drew 33% more fans during the final seven years of the decade than did Yankee Stadium.

New York's Polo Grounds

In the 1960s, baseball's magnetic center shifted West as *Dodger Stadium* held more fans than any other. The jewel of Chavez Ravine held this attendance crown through the 1970s and 1980s.

★ ★ ★ ★ ★

However, in the 1990s, it was the *Skydome in Toronto* that became the belle of the ball.

★ ★ ★ ★ ★

Finally, during the first decade of the 2000s, *the two versions of Yankee Stadium* combined to be the center of the baseball universe. Technically, however, it was *Dodger Stadium* that drew more fans than any other single facility.

54

ODD TEAM NICKNAMES

◇◇

HERE IS A LIST OF SOME OF THE ODDEST TEAM NAMES IN ALL OF MINOR LEAGUE BASEBALL:

- ★ Kannapolis Intimidators
- ★ Asheville Tourists
- ★ Bowling Green
- ★ Lehigh Valley Iron Pigs
- ★ Chattanooga Lookouts
- ★ Fort Myers Miracle
- ★ Traverse City Beach Bums
- ★ Winston-Salem Warthogs
- ★ Lakeland Flying Tigers
- ★ Toledo Mud Hens
- ★ Albuquerque Isotopes
- ★ New Hampshire Fisher Cats
- ★ Rancho Cucamonga Quakes
- ★ Vermont Sea Monsters
- ★ Brevard County Manatees
- ★ Casper Ghosts
- ★ Auburn Doubledays
- ★ Nashville Sounds
- ★ West Virginia Power
- ★ Delmarva Shorebirds
- ★ Hickory Crawdads
- ★ Batavia Muckdogs
- ★ Lakewood Blueclaws
- ★ Lansing Lugnuts
- ★ Long Island Ducks
- ★ Altoona Curve
- ★ Round Rock Express
- ★ Savannah Sand Gnats
- ★ Great Lakes Loons
- ★ Jupiter Hammerheads

★ Inland Empire 66ers of San Bernardino

and finally

★ Montgomery Biscuits

HERE IS A LIST OF SOME OF THE STRANGEST TEAM NAMES FROM THE PAST:

* ★ Kalamazoo Kazoos
* ★ Saginaw-Bay City Hyphens
* ★ Des Moines Prohibitionists
* ★ Columbus Discoverers
* ★ New Haven Nutmegs
* ★ Terra Haute Hottentots

* ★ Dallas Hams
* ★ Rochester Hop Bitters
* ★ Crookston Crooks
* ★ Utica Lunatics
* ★ Sioux City Soos
* ★ Oswego Starchboxes

and

the Walla Walla Walla Wallas

FINALLY, HERE IS A LIST OF BASEBALL TEAMS THAT HAVE NEVER EXISTED, BUT PROBABLY SHOULD HAVE:

* ★ Charlotte Rays
* ★ Dayton Cougars

* ★ Erie Scenarios
* ★ Helena Handbaskets

and

the Macon Loves

THE **ANSWER** TO CHAPTER 52: NAME THAT CLOSER

Dennis Eckersley!

Follies Factoids

I, Rollie Fingers, faced thirty-four batters who would eventually go into the Hall of Fame. Only one managed to post a perfect batting average against me. That player was Steve Carlton.

Nolan Ryan's three most frequent strikeout victims were Claudell Washington (39), Freddy Patek (31), and Jorge Orta (30).

Over the course of their lengthy careers, the famed pitching trio of Tom Glavine, Greg Maddux, and John Smoltz have combined to hit 87 doubles, 6 triples, and 11 home runs.

The Final Follies Challenge

Over the course of my seventeen-year career, I, Rollie Fingers,
faced 927 different hitters during the regular season.

Who was the only one of these 927 hitters
to nick me for as many as 3 career home runs?

The first 75 readers who can e-mail the correct answer
within the subject line to
Yellowstone@baseballprism.com
will win a free one-year e-subscription to our
sister publication *The Baseball Prism* newsletter.
Good luck!!

That's all for now.
Thanks everyone!
I hope you greatly enjoyed *Rollie's Follies*.

~ Rollie Fingers ~

ACKNOWLEDGEMENTS

To the book's skipper *Jack Heffron*,
for his exceptional guidance, expertise, and wisdom.

To *Steve Sullivan*,
for his amazing design and layout of the book.

To *Jerry Dowling*,
for painting with pictures what we could not
with words.

SPECIAL THANKS

The fans and employees of the Arizona Diamondbacks
Tyler Barnes
Stacey Barone
BaseballPrism.com (our sister publication)
Katrina Bevan
Lawrence Bezuska
Rich Bloch
Rick Bosetti
The fans and employees of the Colorado Rockies
Lori Fingers
Kirk Gibson
The Baseball Hall of Fame in Cooperstown, New York
Tom Hardricourt
Conor "Thunderbrows" Jackson
Mac King (the magician)
Allison Lane (the actress)
Major League Baseball
Mike McNally
Tony Migliaccio
The fans and employees of the Milwaukee Brewers
Josh Musselman of the Sonoma State University Seawolves coaching staff
Bryan Pelekoudas
ReelSpiel.com
Sherry Rogelberg
The world's finest literary agent, Dr. Neil Salkind
The fans and employees of the San Diego Padres
Ken Spindler
Studio B
Arnold Topp
Chad Tracy
and Ron Tyler

ORDINARY THANKS
Jim Gantner

SOURCES

Bosetti, Rick. Telephone Interview. (July 14, 2008)

Connor, Floyd. *Baseball's Most Wanted* (Brassey's, 2000)

Connor, Floyd. *Baseball's Most Wanted II* (Brassey's, 2003)

Davids, L. Robert, ed. *Great Hitting Pitchers* (Society for American Baseball Research, Cooperstown, NY, 1979)

Ellis, Edward Robb. *The Epic of New York City* (Carroll & Graf, 1966)

Greenwald, Hank. *This Copyrighted Broadcast* (Woodford Press, 1999)

Hardricourt, Tom. *Brewers Essential* (Triumph Books, 2008)

Jones, Tom. *Working at the Ballpark* (Skyhorse Publishing, 2008)

Silva, Deidre and Koney, Jackie. *It Takes More Than Balls* (Skyhorse Publishing, 2008)

WEBSITE SOURCES

ballparksofbaseball.com
baseball-almanac.com
baseballhalloffame.org
baseballlibrary.com
baseballprospectus.com
baseball-reference.com
baseballreliquary.org
brooklynpaper.com
byrnsie.com
cmgww.com
diamondbacks.scout.com
ericbyrnes.com
espn.com
georgiaencyclopedia.org
hasbro.com
japaneseballplayers.com
imdb.com
mapquest.com
mlb.com
prairesticks.com
spacemanlee.com
sportsillustrated.com
stevetheump.com
thebaseballcube.com
thebaseballpage.com
usatoday.com
westegg.com/inflation
wikipedia.com
yahoo.com/mlb
youtube.com